SEWING ACCESSORIES:
An Illustrated History

Sewing Accessories:
An Illustrated History

Victor Houart

SOUVENIR PRESS

CONTENTS

ACKNOWLEDGEMENTS

I particularly wish to thank Mr Léon Doyen, of the Etablissements Thimonnier in Lyon (France), who built up the collection of sewing machines now in his private museum, the *Musée Thimonnier*, and who was kind enough to provide photographs of all the sewing machines he owns. Special thanks are also due to Mr Jardez, curator of the Folklore Museum at Tournai (Belgium), who helped in many ways, going as far as taking the objects to be photographed to a local studio; and to Mr Ramaekers of the Spa Museum (Belgium), who really went out of his way to provide illustrations.

I should also like to acknowledge the help of the following: Mrs Bridget McConnell, President of the Thimble Society of London, Mrs Darrell J. Turner, of the Singer Company in Guildford, Mr Jean Darbot, of the *Musée de la Bonneterie* in Troyes (France), Mrs Van Hove, antique dealer in Brussels, Miss Cartwright of Bonhams, the London auctioneers, Madame Bériot of Ader, Picard Tajan, Paris auctioneers, Miss Judith Turner, public relations officer of Josiah Wedgwood Ltd., in London, Miss J. Lefranc of the *Musées Royaux d'art et d'histoire* in Brussels, Mr Jacob, the competent editor-in-chief of the Paris magazine *ABC Decor*, and Mr John Read, assistant curator of the Great Yarmouth Museums' Elizabethan House.

Preface

The simple art of sewing may not be as old as the world, but it is at least as old as clothing. When our ancestors discovered that they had to protect themselves against low temperatures, they contrived to cover themselves with suitable animal skins; but those skins had to be put together, and that was the beginning of sewing. Since those prehistoric times sewing has always been a necessary skill and it still is, thousands of years later.

To make life easier for the needlewomen of the past, tools were invented. Some were designed to fulfil specific sewing tasks, and as those tasks, through changing fashion or technological advances, ceased to be performed, the tools were discarded. Some were merely utilitarian and were thrown away by the million, while others, lavishly decorated and beautifully made, were handed down from one generation to the next and many have survived to the present day.

Today, in an age when people are trying to save as much as they can from our past, old sewing tools are collected practically everywhere in Europe and America. There are two kinds of collectors: firstly, those who try to assemble as many old sewing tools as they can, and secondly, those who are attracted to particular categories of objects related to sewing. Some only collect sewing-boxes, others only needle-cases. Thousands of people, the world over, are now collecting nothing but thimbles.

The homely art of sewing has always been part of our lives; yet, strange as it may seem, a complete history of the craft has never been published. There are gaps still to be filled and research to be carried out—difficult research, for historians and diarists of the past have never paid much attention to something that seems so obvious and mundane as to have absolutely no importance for them at all. If, by happy chance, they happened to mention a sewing tool, they invariably neglected to give any specific details. Historians of today are often confronted with old texts, wills or accounts where sewing objects are mentioned, but which, in most cases, are disappointingly vague. And so the gaps in the story remain unfilled. In attempting to trace the history of sewing tools, from the needle to the sewing machine, I have tried to fill as many of these gaps as I could, hoping to add a stone or two to the edifice of our knowledge about this fascinating subject.

Note   Chapter 10 deals with what I have called 'Miscellaneous Sewing Accessories'—such items as reel-boxes, sewing-clamps, and thread waxers. The reader may find it useful to refer to Chapter 10 from time to time for a more detailed description of specific items.

Victor Houart
December 1983

1 NEEDLES AND PINS

Needles

Of all the tools made for sewing, the simplest and yet the most important has always been the modest little needle. Billions of them have been made the world over and billions have been thrown away without the slightest regret. Billions are still being made today to be used in millions of households, but there is hardly a housewife who knows about the origin of this tiny, essential instrument.

The English word 'needle' apparently comes from the Old English *nædl*, which is probably associated with the Latin *nere*, to 'spin'. The root is common to many Teutonic languages, as in Dutch, for instance, where the word for needle is *naald*. The Latins at least are luckier, for they know the etymology of the word they use. The Italians call it *ago* (or *puntina*) and the French call it *aiguille*, both names deriving from the Latin *acus*, meaning 'point'.

Needles, though hitherto of no great interest to historians, are of great antiquity. Right from the beginning of time, prehistoric men, threatened by cold, had to cover themselves, and before they were able to make clothes they used skins. But skins or material had to be sewn together to fit the wearer—and to do that, they required a needle. So as metal was not yet known to them, they used needles made of fishbone, horn or ivory. The Indians and the Chinese consider the needle to be a very ancient instrument—so ancient, they say, that it is impossible to dissociate it from the beginning of the existence of men on earth. The Louvre Museum in Paris has in its collections of prehistoric tools, needles made of iron and bronze, very similar to and no bigger than our modern needles. But although these needles were discovered in Egyptian tombs four thousand years old, they were probably not the first metal needles ever made.

11

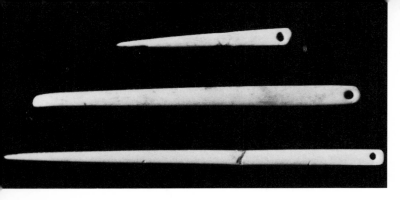

Three bone needles from the paleolithic period, circa 15,000–10,000 BC. *Musées Royaux d'art et d'histoire, Brussels*

Needles of prehistoric origin, with a hole for passing a thread either near the blunt end or in the middle, have been discovered in countless excavations all over Europe—in France, Britain, Italy, Germany—indeed wherever men have lived and died. In fact the bone needle used by our wild and uncivilized ancestors has continued to be made for centuries by all, or nearly all, uncivilized tribes, until not so long ago.

It appears that the very first needle was probably a simple fishbone, flattened at one end and pierced with a hole. The fishbone, if well chosen, was ideal. It was practically a ready-made needle, and with only a little bit of ingenuity it could easily be transformed and used to sew skins together. These early fishbone needles were followed, as time went by and as humanity developed, by needles made of bone or ivory. The first metal needles, made of bronze and similar to the many examples found in most museums, followed in the Bronze Age; and the Egyptians who knew how to produce copper five thousand years ago must have had metal needles even before then. Bronze needles were followed in Western Europe by needles made of other metals such as iron, brass or latten (an alloy usually containing brass or similar yellow metal), which Europeans used intensively until the fourteenth century, when steel needles were introduced from the East. For steel needles, like the art of embroidery, came originally from the East.

All the beautiful fabrics sold in Western Europe in early times came from the Middle East—European women as far back as the fourth century AD contenting themselves with embellishing them with embroidery. They embroidered these Eastern fabrics with

Two bronze needles made in the Bronze Age between the twelfth and eighth centuries BC. *Musées Royaux d'art et d'histoire, Brussels* scenes from the two Testaments and from the lives of the saints. The art of embroidery was supposed, by the Romans, to have been started by the Phrygians. The story was so well established in Roman times that all embroiderers in Rome were called Phrygians. Embroidery became the pastime of noble women as early as the sixth century AD, the art already reaching perfection in the seventh century, particularly in Britain where women were famous for their very precise needlework—a reputation that was maintained throughout the Middle Ages. And those women had to work with inferior quality needles of brass or latten.

Needles are first mentioned in documents of the twelfth century. At the end of the thirteenth, Marco Polo could write that 'the ladies and the young girls work very nobly with needles on silk cloth of all colours, decorating them with beasts, birds and many other pictures.' It was only in the fourteenth century that steel needles started to appear in all European countries, imported from the Middle East, from well known towns which are mentioned again and

A selection of needles and pins dating from the fourteenth to the eighteenth centuries. Copyright ACL Brussels—Namur Museum

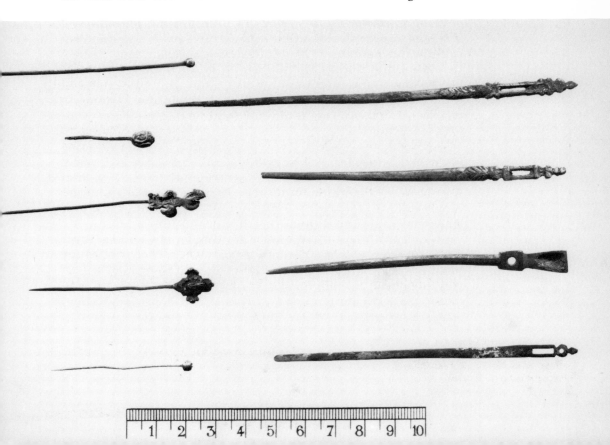

German packet of needles with information printed in Chinese characters.

again in contemporary documents. The needles came mainly from Damascus, the capital of Syria, from Antioch in Asia Minor, and from Adrianople which is the ancient name of Edirne in Turkey, a town which at the time had some five hundred thousand inhabitants and had been the capital of a Latin kingdom started by the Crusaders at the end of the eleventh century. All needles mentioned in contemporary documents are referred to as coming from those three Middle-Eastern towns.

Of course, once they had seen steel needles, the Europeans were not long in producing their own and all historians agree that the first European steel needles were manufactured in the German town of Nuremberg around 1370; but the main manufacturing centres were soon to be located in Italy and Spain, two countries which had links with the Arab world. It took a very long time for these two countries to compete with Moorish production, but once established, at the end of the fifteenth century, their reputation was to last for centuries.

The fact that steel needles were being produced on a grand scale in the East and had started being made in Europe at the end of the fourteenth century does not mean that the other types of needles stopped being manufactured. Steel needles were expensive, so some people still used those made of latten, brass or tin—and for a very long time. But by the sixteenth century steel needles were already very common. Some Europeans were convinced that the best-quality needles came from Cordoba in Spain. Others swore that they could not beat for quality the needles imported from Italy, where they were being manufactured in Milan, Padua and Naples. It was during the sixteenth century that Spanish and Italian production managed to drive out Moorish production almost completely, although needles from Damascus were still imported at the end of that century.

The next century saw the emergence of Britain as a great needle centre, when steel needles were being manufactured in the heart of England—in Redditch in Worcestershire, and in some other small towns in Warwickshire. From then onwards everybody in Europe, starting with the French, wanted to buy and use steel needles imported from England—the famous *aiguilles d'Angleterre* so often mentioned in contemporary French documents. But England had a competitor, Germany, where the town of Aachen had also become an important production centre, with another less important centre in Borcette. British steel needles, exported all over the world, soon replaced Spanish and Italian ones, whose producers could simply not compete with the vast British output. People wanted 'needles from England' and nothing else. Even the French, who were very slow to react against the flow of needles from England, were forced to import their *aiguilles d'Angleterre* and to a lesser degree needles from Germany.

Left: German packet of silver-eyed needles showing Princess Victoria, eldest daughter of Queen Victoria.

Right: Metal holder for packets of needles made by Wavery & Son of Redditch.

France never stood a chance against such competition, and in any case its first needle factory was not opened until 1765, some say by an enterprising Englishman, with English tools and English workers. This first French factory was at Menorval (near L'Aigle, in the Orne département). But even then the Menorval factory produced what they called *aiguilles d'Angleterre*, hoping that buyers would not notice that these so-called English needles were in fact manufactured in France. To try to compete with the emerging British predominance in needle-making, the Germans enlarged their factories at Aachen and Borcette, finding themselves forced to buy machine tools from England with which they produced their own 'English needles', even going so far as to print their advertisements in English. Although at the end of the eighteenth century the French had started other factories in Normandy—at Rouen and Evreux— British needles continued to be imported into France. The majority of needles sold on the continent still came either from England or from Germany, and by the middle of the nineteenth century the world market was dominated by those two nations. The success of the British was not due to the fact that they had better salesmen than the others, but that they had the best machine tools. After having started as a cottage industry in Worcestershire, production developed into a major industry in England much sooner than anywhere else.

Of course, needles are difficult to collect, because in the past they were usually discarded, but a book on sewing accessories would not be complete if it did not include the story of this most ancient of all sewing tools.

Besides the normal sewing needles, many other types are worth studying, for some have been known for centuries. The best known, found in many nineteenth century sewing-boxes, is the bodkin. The strange word 'bodkin', the origin of which is completely unknown, derived apparently from the very early English word 'boidekyn', meaning 'dagger', which in turn could have a very ancient Celtic origin. The French have always used a much more explicit expression to define a bodkin: they call it *aiguille à passer* (needle for threading) or *passe-lacets* (needle for threading laces). In fact, the bodkin is only a needle-like instrument made of bone, iron, steel, silver or gold. It is flat, has one large oblong eye (or sometimes two) through which tape, ribbon, elastic or lace can be passed for threading through a series of loops in the material. It is usually six or seven centimetres long and, unlike a normal sewing needle, it has no sharp point. I have been unable to find out when the bodkin began to be used, but it was already very popular at the beginning of the seventeenth century, when it was made of bone or steel. Silver and gold examples began to appear during the eighteenth century and continued to be made throughout the nineteenth. Although very small, the silver and gold bodkins were always well carved with geometric designs but, unfortunately for the collector, very few are hall-marked. It is still possible to find nineteenth century bodkins made in bone or steel.

Many other types of needle, some only used by the sewing trade, were made well before the seventeenth century, when mercers in all the main European towns were selling, not only the usual sewing needles requested by the ladies, but all kinds of surgical needles and the not so well known 'hair needles'. Few people today are aware that, in the sixteenth and seventeenth centuries, ladies and their hairdressers used a special type of needle known as a 'hair needle' (*aiguille à tête*). It was about ten centimetres long, with a flat head pierced with an oblong eye and a blunt point and, according to seventeenth century documents, it was used by ladies to

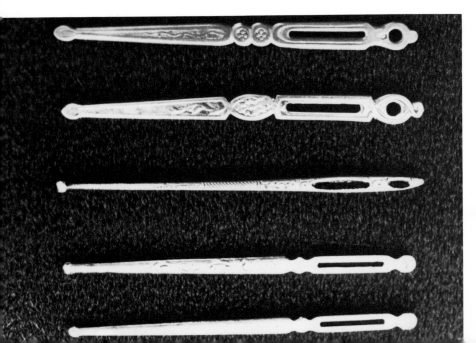

Nineteenth century silver bodkins.

thread and separate strands of hair when they were styling their coiffure.

Upholsterers of the sixteenth and seventeenth centuries also used various types of needle, including the well-known curved upholsterer's needle which is still in use today. From the sixteenth century to the eighteenth, a special needle was used by wigmakers, the wignet needle (*aiguille à réseau*) to make the net base of their wigs. Some documents mention that the wigmaker's needles were split at both ends. They were usually made in iron or in steel. Thick needles in iron or steel were also used by packers as early as the sixteenth century. They were about twelve and a half to fifteen centimetres long, with a round head and a triangular sharp point. Packers used such needles, not to sew clothes, but to sew up their packing canvases with string.

Another needle one might come across was being used by embroiderers well before the seventeenth century for working with gold and silver threads. It was similar in shape to a normal sewing needle, but it was much bigger and had an oblong eye large enough to accommodate the silver threads. French documents from the seventeenth century mention the existence of a special type of needle called *aiguille à soie* (silk needle), similar to but smaller than the bodkin, also with an oblong eye. An even smaller type was the *aiguille à frisure* or *aiguille à bouillon*, used in embroidery and threaded with extremely thin silk to puff material up into relief (as in puff sleeves). It was apparently smaller than the *aiguille à soie* (silk needle). And if one comes across a strong needle with a very wide oblong eye, made of iron or steel, the chances are that it is a string needle which was already being made before the middle of the seventeenth century. All these different types of old needle are sometimes difficult to identify—except perhaps the bodkin from which a very nice collection could be made, specially from the numerous examples in silver and gold which are still to be found.

Needles for mending silk stockings, made in Germany for the French market.

Circular card of pins made by Payton & Iles for the Great Exhibition of 1851. It has an embossed illustration of the Crystal Palace in the centre and a circular inscription: EXHIBITION OF ALL NATIONS 1851. *Courtesy of the Great Yarmouth Museums' Elizabethan House*

Pins

If the needle has been, for thousands of years, a sewing necessity, so has the sewing pin, that insignificant little spike for fastening pieces of fabric together, with one end pointed and the other with a round head. The English word 'pin' comes from the Latin *pinna*, meaning a point. The French word *épingle* derives from the Latin *spinula*, a thorn. And it may well be that the first pin used by man in prehistoric times was none other than a simple thorn, which could be picked up practically anywhere. That the pin is of great antiquity is unquestioned, and one can assume that if cave-dwellers learned to use a needle they soon discovered that a pin was also very useful when sewing. Thorns were replaced by bronze pins during the

Bronze Age, and many, none of them of great archaeological value, have been discovered in excavations. And these bronze pins were replaced, as time went by, by pins of iron, tin or latten.

During the Middle Ages people of a certain standing still had nomadic habits, and when they moved from one place to another they took with them not only their spoons and knives, but furniture, curtains, tapestries and clothes. They also needed pins—a great number, to judge by the evidence of many contemporary documents. For one finds mention of pins in documents as early as the fourteenth century, when people obviously bought a lot of them. The following entry is from the accounts of 1376 of Geoffroi de Fleuri, who was *argentier due roi*, a kind of minister of finance, to Philippe le Long, King of France: 'Celui jour, pour XII milliers de granz espingles pour madame la reine' (Today, for 12,000 pins for the queen). In the same account is an entry referring to another ten thousand pins, bringing the total bought by the Queen of France to twenty-two thousand. Mediaeval pins were made of latten; some unscrupulous characters tried to sell pins made of tin-plate, but the authorities did their best to stop the deception. A document of 1378, now in the National Library of France, refers to this practice in the Paris of the Middle Ages. 'Les jurés espingliers de Paris prindrent en l'ostel de Jehan Biton espinglier, des espingles en fer blanc ou blanchies à grosses têtes et dit le Prévôt de Paris qu'elles n'étaient pas bonnes ne loyales à faire vendre à Paris' (The master pin-makers of Paris took from the house of Jehan Biton, pin-maker, pins made of tin-plate, and the chief magistrate of Paris said that they were not good enough to be sold in Paris).

And from the accounts of 1387 of one of Fleuri's successors, Guillaume Brunel: 'A Jehan le Braconnier, espinglier à Paris, pour ceniers à lui paiez, c'est àssavoir III milliers d'espingles' (To Jehan le Braconnier, pin-maker of Paris, to be paid for 3,000 pins). The name of Jehan le Braconnier (or John the poacher), pin-maker of

Simple pin-box of tin, with a pincushion on its lid.

Like old packets of needles, old pin-boxes showing the maker's name are much sought after by collectors.

Paris, appears in so many Parisian accounts that he must have been in charge of quite a sizeable business right through the fourteenth century. Another mention of this very prolific pin-maker, in a document of 1387: 'A Jehan le Braconnier, espinglier, pour 4 milliers de petites espingles pour l'atour de lad. dame, au prix de 12s. le millier' (To Jehan le Braconnier, pin-maker, for 4,000 pins, for the dresses of the said lady, at a price of 12s. a thousand). And a few years later he is again mentioned: 'A Jehan le Braconnier pour 8 cents espingles courtes de la façon d'Angleterre pour porter devers lad. dame pour l'atour de son chef' (To Jehan le Braconnier for 800 short pins of the English type for the said lady to use in her headgear).

At this time Paris enjoyed a monopoly in pin manufacture, but short pins imported from England must have appeared in the continental shops sometime during the century and must have been well known by 1391, when they were being copied by a man as important as Jehan le Braconnier, supplier to the Court of France. From then on, the *espingles d'Angleterre* are mentioned more and more in French documents. It has been impossible to trace the source of these famous fourteenth century English pins, but what emerges is, as we have seen, that they were sufficiently esteemed to be copied on the continent. It is a pity that contemporary writers were not more explicit and did not give us any descriptions of the pins. They never mention the material they were made of, but it is unlikely that they were made of steel at that time. English imports did not put an end to the production of pins in Paris, as is proved by this

Pin-box with the trade mark of a Belgian maker

entry in the accounts of one Clesse d'Angoûlême, written in 1496:
'Pour 6 milliers d'espingles de Paris, pour mad. et pour
mademoiselle' (For 6,000 pins from Paris, for milady and her
daughter).

Pins made in Paris were sold in France alongside the pins from
England until about the end of the sixteenth century. On the other
side of the Channel, in Britain, pins were also very common during
the Middle Ages, and they too were made of brass or latten. British
output must have increased enormously during the fifteenth century, for the importation of foreign pins was forbidden by law in
1483. Was this because the pin-makers complained and requested
protective measures? Was it because the French exporters tried to
sell their cheap pins made of tin-plated wire in England? England
never allowed these cheap substitutes to be sold on her territory.
But one thing is certain: a few years later French pins were again
allowed into England, though without any danger to British production which had forged ahead and was probably now the most
important in Europe. Paris produced pins for a little while longer,
but slowly their manufacture switched to the provinces, mainly to
L'Aigle in the Orne département and to some towns in Normandy,
where needles were also being produced. These provincial French

pins arrived in Paris in a kind of paper case decorated with the portraits of well-known princes or princesses, landscapes or architectural motifs, and many a French housewife bought the pins more for the decorative container than for the quality of the contents. When the pin-cases were decorated with the portrait of the reigning queen, the pins began to be called *épingles à la reine* (queen's pins).

By the middle of the seventeenth century, the French practically gave up and contented themselves with imported English pins, while some English women still preferred imported French pins. For the French did not cease production altogether, and pins made of latten were still produced in France during the eighteenth century: a kind of cottage industry, each pin still being made by hand instead of manufactured with machine tools, as in England and, of course, Germany. In England also the production of pins had been a kind of cottage industry, but it expanded suddenly when in 1626 a certain John Tilsby opened a pin factory in Stroud (Gloucestershire), soon employing up to fifteen hundred workers. Ten years later the first guild of pin-makers was created in London. This dealt the final blow to French production: the Paris workshops closed for good, and during the eighteenth century there was only a small output in L'Aigle and in Normandy. Starting in Stroud, British production moved first to Bristol as a main centre, then to London and later, of course, to Birmingham.

It is difficult to know how these old pins were made and what they looked like, except that they had a round head and came in various sizes. Up to about the middle of the nineteenth century they were made in two parts with the head formed from a coil of metal twisted round the shaft. Thereafter they started to look exactly like the pins we use today, which are made in a single piece of metal. Of course, during the second half of the nineteenth century some pins were already made in blue or slightly purple steel, and even black—for no particular reason, except that black pins were very popular for mourning, for nineteenth century women often wore black clothes, and ordinary steel pins would have been too conspicuous. Up to the First World War, pins as well as needles had a tendency to rust very quickly, so then they were made of stainless steel. They are still made today in that material, and the pins we are using now will probably never change.

2   PIN- AND NEEDLE-HOLDERS

~~~~~~

Pincushions and emery-cushions

Before the First World War, housewives, seamstresses and tailors always had an emery-cushion handy when they were sewing. Before the manufacture of stainless steel needles, the old steel needles had a regrettable tendency to rust very easily, and once rust had appeared it was practically impossible to use them, especially when sewing very fine material like silk. Housewives had to face the hard fact that either they could throw the rusty needles away and buy new ones, with all the expense that that would entail, or they could derust them with the help of an emery-cushion—which is what most of them did.

The emery-cushion looks exactly like a pincushion, although some say that it was a bit smaller—which is yet to be proved. The only real difference between the two was that the pincushion, made to hold pins and needles and protect them against rust, was filled with some light material like cotton wool, while the emery cushion was filled with emery powder: and while the pincushion was meant to prevent rusting, the emery-cushion actually removed rust. The rusty needle or pin could be stuck in the emery-cushion and jiggled up and down in the emery powder until all traces of rust had disappeared. It was a great help, but once a needle had started to rust really badly, nothing much could be done about it. Makers of pincushions also made emery-cushions, using the same type of container for both.

Pincushions—or pin pillows as they were sometimes called— have a very long history, and were already in use during the fourteenth century. The oldest known text referring to a pincushion, the inventory of a Frenchwoman, Yolande de Bar, is dated 1361; one of the entries refers to 'un coussinet où il y a plein

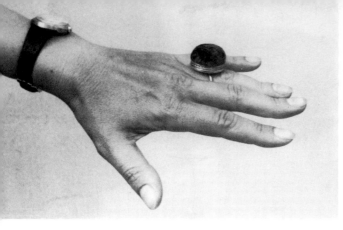

de grosses épingles d'or' (a little cushion in which big gold pins are stuck). In French mediaeval documents one finds many references to *espingliers*, which could mean a pin-box or a pincushion. The most interesting reference to an early pincushion is of 1492, in a book written by a certain Olivier de la Marche and called *Parement des dames* (*Ladies' adornment*). The description is quite vivid:

Un tabouret qu'on dit espinglier
Pour mieux être ma maîtresse assortie
La ceinturette en doit être garnie
Cet espinglier doit avoir couverture
D'un beau drap d'or pour princesse servir
De drap de laine doit être la bordure
Pour des espingles recevoir la poincture.

A little poem without importance, perhaps, for those who are not interested in sewing tools—which could be translated as follows:

A tiny stool called a 'pin-holder'
To better suit my mistress
Must be suspended from her little belt,
Such a pin-holder must have a cover
Made out of gold cloth fit for a princess.
The border must be of woollen cloth
To receive the pricking of the pins.

It would be hard to find a better description of a fifteenth century pincushion. Olivier de la Marche also makes a point of telling us that fifteenth century women carried their pincushions with them,

25

suspended from their belts. And what was true of France must have been true of anywhere else in Europe. Very often reported as being in use from the mid-seventeenth century onwards, pincushions were in fact common during the Middle Ages, at least as far back as the fourteenth century, as in 1361 when Yolande de Bar, as we have already seen, used a pincushion to hold her gold pins.

Because the French word *espinglier* could mean pincushion or pin-box, references in old documents are not clear as to whether cushion or box is meant, except when the word 'box' is added. Another French writer, Philippe Monet, could, however, boldly state in 1635 that an *espinglier* was a 'small cushion to hold pins'—which does not settle the question, as the French continued well after the seventeenth century to call their pin-boxes *espingliers*.

Be that as it may, the pincushion was very common almost everywhere from the seventeenth century onwards. Rather large rectangular, embroidered pincushions were very popular in England during the seventeenth century. They were lavishly decorated with all kinds of designs, particularly flowers, in silk or metal thread. And it was in the same century that pincushions started to be studded with pins arranged in a pattern, in the form of a message or a date. In most cases they were made of linen. It is probable that such pincushions were given as wedding or christening presents until well into the nineteenth century. From the eighteenth century until the First World War pincushions of knitted silk, often filled with cotton wool and decorated with names and mottoes, were given as presents, some of them being manufactured. In the nineteenth century, and only in Britain, soldiers and sailors offered their girlfriends pincushions, which were often heart-shaped and decorated with glass-headed pins, messages and pictures. It seems that sailors and soldiers of other countries were less romantic than their British counterparts and never indulged in the practice.

Pincushions not incorporated in any kind of container are diffi-

Pincushion made by a soldier of the East Lancashire regiment for his love, decorated with glass-topped pins and beads. *Courtesy of the Kay Shuttleworth Collection Trust*

cult to find, for they were made of perishable material and never lasted long. Collectors have a better chance with the pincushions made in fanciful shapes, in wood or metal, from the middle of the eighteenth century, which were in general use during Victorian times in practically all countries. It is impossible to catalogue them all, as new ones always seem to be appearing on the market. Most of the fanciful pincushion containers were made in the shape of fruit (mainly strawberries), flowers, baskets, shoes of various sizes, wheelbarrows, dolls, all kinds of animals (with pigs and rabbits as favourites) and birds. Wooden containers were often in the form of shoes or little stools—one of the most ancient kinds as we have seen, already in existence during the Middle Ages. Ivory was used as well as wood and some delightful pincushions are to be found enclosed in delicately carved ivory baskets. Silver and gold pincushions were also made during the nineteenth century, but they belong, of course, to the luxury class and do not turn up very often. They too would be in all the usual forms such as animals, birds and shoes. In fact all the shapes that cheap pincushions were made in can be found in silver. Some pincushions are rarer than others; some were even decorated with Wedgwood jasper ware cameos. These rare pincushions were made of octagonal-section polished wood, with a hinged lid set with a blue and white cameo under glass, the interior being fitted with a velvet pincushion.

A very attractive type of pincushion to be found on the continent, mainly in France, was the statuette pincushion, which was made between the end of the eighteenth century and the beginning of the nineteenth. The most attractive ones were beautiful Louis XV marquesses carved in wood, with characteristic tall headgear. The top of the headgear was hollow and contained the pincushion. French women of the eighteenth century also used plain little cloth dolls as pincushions.

The pinwheel, made out of two flat discs enclosing a narrow pincushion, was another type. They were produced for sale at seaside resorts and spa towns all over Europe, and were very popular as souvenirs. The two discs of the seaside pinwheel were more often

Left: Cat-shaped pincushion, a popular nineteenth century design, in silver-coloured metal. *Margaret Kinnear Collection*

Right: From Yugoslavia, a pincushion in a small leather shoe. *Margaret Kinnear Collection*

than not made of mother-of-pearl and inscribed with the name of the resort; others were made of wood decorated with tiny shells, always with the name of the resort inscribed in some suitable spot.

At the end of the nineteenth century many pincushions were made incorporating porcelain half-figures. These half-figures, made only by the numerous German porcelain factories, served many purposes. Fitted with skirts, they were used as teacosies; they covered telephones and they decorated powder-puffs, as well as pincushions. Porcelain pincushions are not at all rare. They come in the familiar shapes of baskets, birds and animals. Particularly appealing were those made in the form of swans of different sizes.

There were three principal souvenir ware industries that made pincushions: the first one was Spa in Belgium, followed by Tunbridge Wells, then Mauchline in Scotland. There is almost no end to the variety of pincushions, for during the nineteenth century they were made in bone and papier mâché as well as the other materials already mentioned. Some of the most beautiful were made in enamelled silver by Russian silversmiths in the old Russian style, including the very expensive ones made at the end of the nineteenth century by the well known Russian goldsmith Carl Fabergé.

Note Collectors should bear in mind that every pincushion could in fact conceal an emery-cushion, which went out of fashion in the early 1920s when needles and pins were made in stainless steel and did not rust any more.

Home-made hat-shaped needle cases in crochet, each containing a thimble. Early 1920s. *Margaret Kinnear Collection*

Other kinds of pin-holder

The word pin-holder applies to anything made to hold pins, and that includes, of course, the pincushion. The pincushion was strictly utilitarian, and needlewomen always kept one handy while sewing. But pincushions were not the only type of holder available in the old days. The other common type was more often than not the little box, in which the needlewoman could safely keep her pins. Pin-boxes were in use all over Europe during the Middle Ages. The various forms they took during that period are never fully described in documents, but some texts are reasonably explicit.

Pin-boxes are already to be found as early as 1360, in the inventory of a certain Jeanne de Boulogne in France: '2 espingliers battus en or à un lion de pelles d'une part et un aigle d'autre part' (Two pin-boxes in gold with a lion on one side and an eagle on the other). The description is rather vague, but it shows incontestably that pin-boxes of the luxury type existed during the fourteenth century. Jeanne de Boulogne's inventory fortunately contains another entry which would gladden the heart of any historian: 'Une boîte d'argent à mettre espingles à la façon d'une poire' (A silver box in the shape of a pear to keep pins in). Nothing could be more precise and revealing. Jeanne de Boulogne was the lucky owner of at least two beautiful pin-boxes, and it can be assumed that she was not the first to own such pieces, for others must have been made much earlier.

A few years later, in 1376, the will of Avice de la Monteure mentions that the lady leaves to a dear friend 'her good sapphire, her prayer books and her *silver pin-box*'. Even more striking is a description in the inventory of the possessions of Marie de Sully, written in 1409: the entry states that she owned 'un espinglier d'argent entour duquel sont le crucifiement, Saint-Pierre, Saint-Paul et les armes du pape Urbain VI' (a silver pin-holder around which are represented the crucifixion, St Peter, St Paul and the arms of Pope Urban VI). It must have been a pin-box quite out of this world! It seems that expensive, luxury pin-boxes were not so rare during the Middle Ages, and some of them must have been even more beautiful than the one owned by Marie de Sully. As early as 1380 quite a few pin-boxes are reported as 'espingliers taillés en émaux' (pin-boxes decorated with enamel).

All the evidence from mediaeval documents indicates that early pin-boxes were square or rectangular, with a hinged lid. The elongated pin-boxes referred to as *étuis* began to appear at the end of the fifteenth century. The French word *étui*, used in English as well as in French, derives from the old verb *estuier*, to keep inside or lock away. The word appears in many wills written in French, but it has been impossible to discover when it was adopted in England. In the inventory of Charlotte d'Albret (1514) one reads that she had 'two estuys for comb and a pair of scissors'. The word was in general use in the seventeenth century, and was applied to 'those little tubes meant to keep needlework tools'. Jacques Savary des Bruslons (1657–1718), inspector of workshops in Paris (a sort of customs official), gives us the best contemporary description in his famous *Dictionnaire Universel du Commerce, d'histoire naturelle, d'arts et métiers* which was translated into English in 1774: 'the *étuis* for toothpicks, needles and pins are small hollow cylinders with a lid, in which tools for the toilette and for sewing are kept. Some are made of gold, some of silver, or are decorated with little studs of these two metals. Others are of wood or ivory, and some are made of cardboard covered with leather.' The pin-holders or *étuis* of the sixteenth and seventeenth centuries were usually of leather, either plain or decorated; or of carved ivory or bone, the sumptuous types mentioned in wills and inventories being in fact few and far between. In many cases the *étuis* matched the scissor-holders.

Right from the beginning of the seventeenth century, the pin-holders of the rich were fabulous. They were made of gold, silver or silver gilt, and sometimes decorated with precious stones and enamels. In France such luxury items attracted the eyes of the law, first in 1664 and then in 1692. Henceforth *étuis* were to be taxed according to the materials they were made of: pin-holders in gold, silver and silver gilt were simply taxed as jewellery, and the others

Pin-box in Andenne porcelain. Second half of the nineteenth century. *Author's collection*

much less drastically. At the time of the first tax imposition, *étuis* were made of gold or silver, chiselled or engraved, decorated with enamels or precious stones; they were also made of ivory and of precious or scented woods. But already some were made of simple steel.

Notwithstanding the heavy duty, luxury pin-holders and needle-holders continued to be made throughout the eighteenth century, and many goldsmiths of the period designed and produced lavishly decorated ones. In the eighteenth century, the golden age of French decorative arts, one could still acquire in the fashionable Paris shops pin-holders not only of gold, silver, ivory or scented woods, but also of tortoiseshell, steel, *vernis Martin* and shagreen.

Vernis Martin and shagreen pin-boxes were typical of the eighteenth century. *Vernis Martin* was an imitation lacquer, not actually invented by the four Martin brothers, who gave their name rather to the technique of lacquering. Lacquer was not an eighteenth century invention; the British had already produced imitation lacquer during the second decade of the seventeenth century, and by the end of that century it was being made everywhere—in France, England, Germany, Denmark and Belgium. Before the Martin brothers first produced their famous lacquer in 1745, lacquered objects were already very common in Europe. In the famous Gobelins, in Paris, there was in 1713 a special workshop charged with the production of 'ouvrages de la Chine en peinture et dorure pour le Roi'. Its director was Jacques Dagly from Spa, the brother of Gérard Dagly who had invented Spa varnish. The main achievement of the Martin brothers was that, in 1748 or thereabouts, when their factory became a royal establishment, they ceased to imitate Chinese and Japanese lacquer and produced lacquer in the French style. They stopped copying the Orientals, and instead of covering their products with little Chinese people, pagodas and strange-looking trees from the East, they covered them with typically French scenes. Others adopted the idea, and it is now impossible to say whether the lacquer was made in one of the brothers' three factories in Paris or by other cabinetmakers. Many needle-holders and pin-holders in *vernis Martin* are found today, always decorated with scenes inspired by the painters of the French eighteenth century school—Boucher, Fragonard, Liotard and others. All such holders were produced during the second half of the eighteenth century.

Apart from the *vernis Martin* pin-boxes of the cylinder type, the eighteenth century also produced some beautiful pin-boxes in shagreen. The word 'shagreen' comes from the French *chagrin*; originally it was a kind of dyed leather made from the skin of a shark. In the eighteenth century, the French called it *roussette* (a kind of dogfish) or *galucha* (or *galuchat*), after the name of the man reputed to have invented it. Later in the century they called it *peau de chagrin*. The French have always said that the use of shagreen began in France, basing their case on a book published in 1778, *Les tablettes royales du Vrai Mérite*, in which one reads: 'Galuchat the father, residing on the quai des Morfondus in Paris, was the first to have discovered the art of softening the roussette and shark skins and dying them with colours.' Be that as it may, shagreen was used to cover countless boxes during the second half of the eighteenth century, and most of them were green.

During the second half of the nineteenth century people could buy porcelain pin-boxes, always simply and charmingly made, in all the fairs and markets of Britain and the Continent. Some appear to have been made in Staffordshire, but there is some doubt about their provenance, and most are thought to have been made by the porcelain firm of Conta and Boehme, of Pössneck in Saxony. Some are marked with the characteristic concave shield with the bent arm pointing upwards, although this trade mark is sometimes attributed to Elbogen in Bohemia. But most of these delightful pin-boxes in hard-paste porcelain, with lids decorated with figures or little groups, are unmarked. Many were in fact made at Andenne in Belgium, where up to eight porcelain factories were active during the nineteenth century, producing millions of porcelain objects including statuettes of all the saints to be found in the calendar. Miniature groups, some of them allegorical, were often put on top of the pin-boxes. The Andenne factories were very important, mainly during the second half of the century, when up to half a million items were made and sold in one year. There was a great vogue for them, particularly between 1850 and 1880. Andenne pin-boxes and other items are liable to appear anywhere, but as they are unmarked and as few experts, even, are familiar with Andenne

German nineteenth century porcelain pin-box.

ware, these delightful pieces are often attributed to German factories they had nothing to do with.

Andenne porcelain is in fact recognizable by the paste and the various colours used. There is nothing more charming than those little porcelain pin-boxes, with their miniature groups or single figures decorating the lids. The earlier examples are better made, with more careful modelling and more delicate colours. Assembling a good collection of that type of pin-box alone would probably take a lifetime—which suits the serious collector perfectly.

Needle-holders

Once women had needles and pins, the need to find a suitable holder to keep them safely soon arose. Needles and pins were such elusive objects, so small and thin, that they always had a tendency to disappear from view. Needles were expensive items long ago, as the various old accounts still extant reveal. And so the needle-holder, or *aiguillier* as the French used to call it, was invented. The needle-holder of the Middle Ages was quite a different object from the much later, cylindrical, *étui*. The mediaeval needle-holder, like many other items, was supposed to be carried attached to the belt of the owner. Women must have been quite a sight with their needle-

Hollow ivory statuettes were often used as needle holders from the Middle Ages until the eighteenth century.

holders, key-holders, scissor-holders and other utilitarian objects always attached to their belts. All these separate holders were to be replaced by the *châtelaine*, but not until the second half of the eighteenth century.

The commonest mediaeval needle-holder was diamond-shaped and made of a strong material such as ivory, gold, silver or wood, sometimes lavishly decorated, but often they were made of plain strong leather. Gold and silver ones were chiselled or engraved and sometimes decorated with enamel, and they sometimes carried inscriptions and mottoes. The diamond-shaped cover had a hole in one of its sharp angles large enough to let a fine chain or a twisted cord pass through. A few pieces of suitable fabric, cut in diamond shapes the same size as the cover, were attached to the chain, and the needles were pinned to the fabric. To get hold of a needle, the owner only had to pull the pieces of fabric down from the protective cover, take the needle she wanted and then pull the fabric up. That system has always been used, and even today key-holders of that type are still being made.

The cover, which had to match the standing of its owner, was often of the luxury type, but the poorer people had to make do with the much simpler leather cases, also diamond-shaped (the reason for the shape is obscure). Between the luxury needle-holders and the simple leather models was to be found yet another diamond-shaped holder, this one made of strong fabric richly decorated with pearls or embroidery in gold or silver thread. This type of needle-holder remained fashionable until well into the sixteenth century.

Needle-holders are mentioned in documents as early as the twelfth century, but no indication as to their form is given. In the famous *Roman de la Rose*, published around 1300, we find:

Lors trais une aiguille d'argent
D'un aiguillier mignot et gent.
(She then pulled a silver needle
From a needle-holder charming and fine.)

We know little of the industrial disturbances of fourteenth-century Paris, but there is evidence of a serious row between the mercers who were selling needle-holders and the silversmiths who were making them. Reports of the row reveal that needle-holders were very common and very richly decorated, the main complaint of the silversmiths being that mercers were selling needle-holders in gold and silver, decorated with precious stones: since the silversmiths made them, they felt they should be the ones to sell them. The fourteenth-century document points out that 'ils demandent l'imposition de teux aiguilliers de soie, d'or, d'argent, respondent les orfèvres que ce la couverture de l'aiguillier était d'or et d'argent ou garny de pierreries, que c'est l'orfèvre et les font les orfèvres et non pas les merciers.' The silversmiths objected, quite rightly, to the mercers selling holders in gold and silver, decorated with precious stones. The dispute is a mere isolated incident, but it confirms that needle-holders were quite common in the fourteenth century and that some were extremely lavish and fine—belonging, of course, to the very rich of the period, and it was not everybody who could be the owner of 'un aiguillier en drap de laine à couches de soie et à menues pierreries des Indes' (a needle-holder in wool, with silk leaves and decorated with tiny stones from India), as indicated in a will dated 1391. If the diamond-shaped holder was the main type used throughout the Middle Ages, the well known cylinder type, very often in carved ivory, was already in existence in the fifteenth century. It was the prototype of the bodkin-case, which was made until the end of the nineteenth century.

References to needle-holders are plentiful all down the centuries, and can be found in countless wills and inventories. In 1534, in the royal accounts of the King of France (Comptes des bâtiments du roi) one finds, for instance, this superb entry: 'A Jehan le Grain, marchand, joaillier et lapidaire demeurant à Paris, un esguillier de cristal garny de rubis et de turquoises' (To Jehan le Grain, merchant, goldsmith and lapidary, residing in Paris, one needle-holder in crystal decorated with rubies and turquoises). Such a needle-holder would probably be worth a fortune today. When, in 1561, they decided to draw up the inventory of the castle at Pau in southern France, they found there 'un esguillier d'ébène garny d'argent, un autre esguillier d'argent esmaillé de noir, au autre esguillier fait à jour de fil tiré' (an ebony needle-holder decorated with silver, another needle-holder in silver enamelled in black (perhaps niello silver) and another holder in filigree silver). During the course of the sixteenth century, the diamond-shaped needle-holder slowly

Typical diamond-shaped needle-book made throughout the Middle Ages in decorated ivory, wood or metal.

disappeared, to be replaced by a similar holder, still equipped with a pull-up chain or cord, but square. It was fashionable during the period to have needle-holders made of strong cardboard covered with tooled leather or with velvet of various colours, heavily embroidered with gold or silver thread. These velvet covers were also made for other purposes, and some contained perfume bottles.

The seventeenth century saw other types of needle-holders lavishly made in gold, silver, silver gilt, ivory, scented woods and even steel. Most were cylindrical, a type that had begun to be made at the end of the fifteenth century. Some were already being made in the form of little square or rectangular boxes. The cylindrical type reached its peak during the eighteenth century, when many were made not only in precious metals but also in wood, enamel and ivory, and also in the two new materials, *vernis Martin* and shagreen.

But the eighteenth century was particularly the period of the flat, rectangular *étuis*. The *étui*, sometimes misspelled in English as 'etwee', was a small case in which objects such as needles could be kept. Contemporary goldsmiths produced some extraordinary examples of the type, which are nowadays beyond the reach of the small collector. The French designer Meissonnier drew some exquisite designs which were often reproduced by the Parisian goldsmiths. The *étui* was usually hung on the eighteenth-century

Four eighteenth century needleboxes. *Left to right:* in vernis Martin, with birds and insects on a gold background; in soft paste Mennecy porcelain painted with flowers and foliage; in varicoloured gold, of Swiss origin; in Meissen porcelain, gold-mounted, with flowers and golden foliage. *Courtesy of Ader Picard Tajan, Paris*

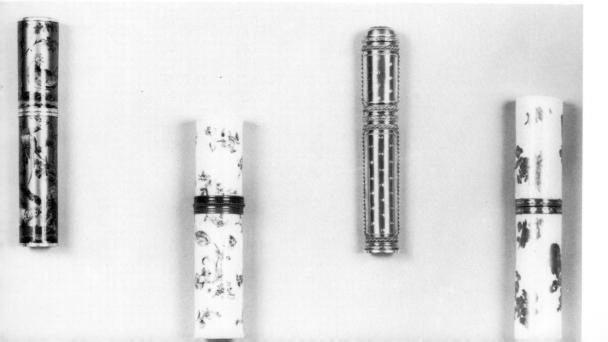

Left: Continental blue ground enamel étui decorated with scenes and flowers. Late eighteenth century. *Courtesy of Bonhams, London*

Right: Eighteenth century needlecase in carved ivory. *Musées Royaux d'art et d'histoire, Brussels*

lady's *châtelaine* (see Chapter 5), the hinged lid of the *étui* being held by a press-button catch. If the majority of gold *étuis* are of continental origin, the British are the only ones to have produced them in pinchbeck, during the second half of the eighteenth century. This was an alloy resembling gold and containing about five parts of copper to two of zinc. Invented by a British clockmaker called Pinchbeck, the alloy was given his name.

Marvellous *étuis* in porcelain mounted on gold, silver or cheaper metals were also produced during the second half of the eighteenth century, by the main European porcelain manufacturers such as Sèvres, Meissen and Tournai. Most are decorated with *genre* scenes or with flowers. Some rarer ones from the last quarter of the century were decorated with silhouettes of women's heads. Quite a lot of them carry inscriptions or mottoes expressing love or friendship. In the well known Parisian shop called 'Au Petit Dunkerque', frequented by royalty, one could choose from a vast assortment: tortoiseshell, shagreen, ivory, scented wood, steel, engraved and enamelled gold, and *vernis Martin*. Most of the eighteenth-century cylindrical needle-holders in *vernis Martin* are decorated with rustic

Nineteenth century Chinese silver needle holder. *Prince Philippe Antiques Collection, Brussels*

or silvan scenes inspired by contemporary paintings of the French school, such as those by Boucher, Fragonard, Perronneau and Watteau. These holders can still be found, with a bit of luck, at a reasonable price. Other cylindrical needle-holders were also produced in Spa wood during the second quarter of the century. They were painted with scenes of flowers, in gouache or watercolour, and were highly varnished. Most carry inscriptions in French, often misspelled. The shagreen needle-holders are rarer than those in Spa wood or *vernis Martin*, though they are mentioned in many eighteenth-century wills. Marie-Josèphe de Saxe, who was the mother of three kings—Louis XVI, Louis XVIII and Charles X—was the owner of an 'embroidery needle, in crystal decorated with gold, kept in an *étui* of galucha (shagreen)'.

Some of the nicest needle-holders of the eighteenth century, both of the flat, rectangular type and of the cylindrical type, were produced in painted or transfer-printed enamels, always lavishly decorated with scenes, portraits or flowers. In England as well as on the continent, these holders are often referred to as Battersea enamel, on account of a very famous English enamel works installed in York House, Battersea, on the south bank of the Thames, which produced delightful transfer-painted enamel trinkets between 1753 and 1756, when it went bankrupt. Similar enamel holders were of course also produced in Germany, Switzerland and France. But in England the most prolific enamel centres were located far from Battersea, in Bilston and Wednesbury, in South Staffordshire, and, of course, in Birmingham.

Most of the ivory holders were probably produced in the town of Dieppe, which had become known for its carved ivories as early as the fourteenth century, when sailors brought back ivory from Africa. With such a good and regular supply of ivory, the people of Dieppe started making the small objects which are now so much sought after. Dieppe was considered the European centre for carved ivories in the sixteenth and seventeenth centuries, when they produced beautiful boxes, knife handles, statues of Christ and the Virgin Mary, and groups on ebony bases. In the eighteenth century, and probably earlier, they made delicate cylindrical needle-holders, thimble-cases and thimbles.

The collector has an enormous choice when it comes to the

38

nineteenth century, for both cylindrical and flat, rectangular needle-cases continued to be made in ivory, porcelain, enamel, bone and wood, sometimes decorated with piqué work or inlaid with gold. Of course, needle-books, with the two sides beautifully painted or decorated with transfers, were made as souvenirs. Spa produced these, together with cylindrical holders of various sizes. Some of the cylindrical ones could be unscrewed to reveal a second case for thimbles. Some rarer examples are in the form of two or four spools. Needle-books were made in Tunbridge Wells, and the Scottish souvenir ware of Mauchline included quite a lot in sycamore decorated with transfers depicting all kinds of locations, even continental ones. And it was the nineteenth century, once again, that produced the novelty design—cases in such shapes as shoes, umbrellas, church spires and pea-pods. Some large ones in the form of musical instruments were made at the very end of the century. The First World War marked the end of the luxury type of needle-holder, and thereafter more utilitarian cases in wood or leather were produced.

It is impossible to catalogue all the many kinds of needle-case that have been made through the centuries, as unknown types are liable to appear any day. But the needle-case offers the collector enormous scope, expenditure of time and money—so long as one is content with the more ordinary specimens, for there is a huge difference between a utilitarian case of the nineteenth century and a beautiful eighteenth-century luxury needle-case, which will fetch a high price. Fortunately, cases in *vernis Martin*, shagreen and Spa wood can still be found, with a bit of luck.

Needlecases of the nineteenth century, in ivory, metal and wood. *Folklore Museum, Tournai*

3 THIMBLES AND THIMBLE-HOLDERS

Thimbles

It did not take long, once the needle had been invented, for people to discover that the finger was rather too soft to push it through tough material. The needle hurt and the finger had to be protected. So, with characteristic human ingenuity, someone thought of making a thimble, a small hollow cylinder to cover the top of the pushing finger. After that, thimbles never ceased to be made, and they are still made today the world over, in a great variety of materials and decorative finishes. Today thimble-collecting can be an absorbing hobby. And unless one is looking for the rare types—those in porcelain bearing the crossed swords of Meissen or the entwined 'L's of Sèvres, or the enamelled thimbles of Fabergé—examples are plentiful. For thimbles have been produced by the billion.

There are two main kinds—first, the near-conical or dome-topped thimbles everybody knows, then the thimble that took the simple form of a band, leaving the top of the finger exposed. Both are embossed or indented round the side and occasionally on top. Only the first type, which covered the tip of the finger, has been made in all kinds of materials, cheap and expensive, and decorated in many different ways. The second type appears to have been made only in cheap metals, and was basically utilitarian. The thimble owes its name to the fact that originally some were worn on the thumb: hence they have also been called thumbells, thumbles, thymels and even thummies. In France, which became a great producer of thimbles, the open or band type was called a *deau* until the eighteenth century, the other type being called a *dé* from the Latin *digitus* meaning 'finger'. There is no doubt that the Romans used thimbles, for open-ended thimbles have been found in the ruins of Herculaneum, buried in 79 AD by the eruption of Vesuvius. Examples of the closed-end kind have been found in other excavations. The Roman thimble, made of bronze, iron, gold or ivory, was shaped like a rounded cone or an olive.

The Romans probably passed their information to the Celts whom they had conquered, for many Gallo-Roman thimbles have also been found, usually in the shape of a pitted cone and made in bronze. It is known that in the twelfth century ordinary people and servants used thimbles made of leather called 'polliceums' or 'digitals'. One finds references to thimbles in thirteenth century texts, notably in the famous register of Etienne Boileau, who was *prévôt* or head of the Parisian merchants and craftsmen. The register, which dates from 1260, contains references to all the guilds in Paris, including some to the latten workers: 'Nus du mestier de frémailleurs de laiton, dessusd ne puet faire *deux* pour home ou pour femme establis à coudre, qui ne soient bons et loyaux, bien marchéans, de bon etoffe, c'est à savoir de bon laiton et de fer' (We latten-workers cannot make thimbles for men or women engaged in the profession of sewing, that are not good and reliable, that is to say of good material, of latten or of iron).

So we know that one category of craftsmen were making thimbles in iron and latten. We also know that buttonmakers were making them in brass or in archal, a strange mediaeval metal about which we know little except that it was not unlike brass. Another early mention is found in the *Dit des Merciers*, a collection of proverbs and popular expressions from the thirteenth century, where we find: 'J'ai des déeus de costurières' (I have seamstress's thimbles). And in a letter written in 1389, discovered by the French historian Carpentier, there is a mention of a *dei à couldre* (a sewing thimble). Unfortunately, all thirteenth-century texts omit to mention the details we would most like to have—an actual description. The fifteenth-century texts are a little clearer: in the accounts of Queen

Four early thimbles. *Left to right:* Mid fifteenth century brass, hand punched; late fourteenth century brass tailor's thimble; late fifteenth or early sixteenth brass; Nuremberg thimble with decorated band. *Courtesy of the Thimble Society of London*

Mother-of-pearl
thimble, about 1800.
*Courtesy of the
Thimble Society of
London*

Charlotte, second wife of Louis XI of France, one entry goes as follows: 'To the said Mathelin Forget, merchant at Amboise, for Epinay thread, needles and thimbles to be used in the rooms of the said lady'. In the same account, written in 1483, one reads that Queen Charlotte also had, 'in a box of white wood, gloves from Catalunya, thimbles from Milan and needles'.

Common mediaeval thimbles were made of iron, brass, or latten, and they already had the modern shape of flat or domed top, but they were always indented by hand. The indentations are therefore very irregular—always a good sign for the collector. From the fourteenth century onwards, thimbles began to be decorated with the coats of arms of their owners, and some particularly interesting examples adopted the shape of an *heaume*, the totally enveloping mediaeval helmet worn by knights. There is one of that type in a great private collection.

It appears that it was not until the sixteenth century that sumptuous and expensive thimbles started being produced, in gold and silver, and very often embellished with precious stones. The inventory of the King of Navarre's jewels, written in 1583, records that the king owned 'a small black wooden box, containing two gold thimbles decorated with rubies'. Similar luxury thimbles were produced throughout Europe during this century, including England; one famous thimble that is often mentioned is the one belonging to Queen Elizabeth I that she was supposed to have given to a lady-in-waiting. It was in gold set with rubies and sapphires. If the King of Navarre could afford such luxuries, no doubt the Queen of England could too.

It was also during this time that thimbles in silver or cheaper metals started to be decorated with relief scroll patterns, which replaced the normal indentations. At the same time a number of beautiful thimbles were being produced in France, Germany and Italy, made of gold or silver and engraved along their edges with all kinds of mottoes and messages, such as:

Prenez-le en gré. (Accept this with pleasure.)
De bon coeur, je le donne. (I give it gladly.)

As the inscriptions are always in French, it is rather difficult to attribute a nationality to these delightful thimbles. The following

42

inscription appears on a German silver thimble, hallmarked in 1587: 'A ce présent est jointe ma meilleure pensée' (To this gift I add my best wishes)—proof, again, that inscribed thimbles were given as presents as early as the sixteenth century. In fact they were given as presents to brides and young mothers before this time, and the practice of offering thimbles on special occasions continued until the beginning of the twentieth century.

We should bear in mind that up to the end of the sixteenth century thimbles were still imported from the Middle East, and that the famous towns which made our very first steel needles also made the thimbles to go with them. Many of those lovely thimbles from Turkey, Syria and Persia, from Damascus or Andrinople, are now in private collections. But, as with the needle industry, by the end of the fifteenth century, the main production centres had shifted from the Middle East to Italy and Spain and many thimbles were exported by Milan and Cordoba throughout the sixteenth century.

The thimbles from Persia were particularly beautiful; in a certain private collection in Paris there is, for instance, a huge one in the form of a mosque, which was probably used by rugmakers. Another sixteenth-century Persian thimble is in gold, engraved with foliage and decorated in enamel with a Persian miniature. A third, also in gold, is decorated with birds and palms on a black enamel background, indentations appearing only on the top. One of the most beautiful in the same private collection, and also from sixteenth-century Persia, is in the form of a tiara, made of gold and set with tiny rubies.

The seventeenth century produced some remarkable thimbles, but it is very difficult in Britain to find thimbles made before the Civil War, most of the extant English examples being of the eighteenth century. The habit of decorating thimbles with inscrip-

Silver thimbles in various sizes, the smallest being used as a charm.

Eighteenth century
French silver thimble.

tions continued throughout the century. As well as silver and gold, thimbles were made of cheaper metals, wood or bone, and were sometimes decorated not only with inscriptions but also with precious stones and enamel. One type of thimble of the period is peculiar to France: it was made in coconut wood with a top and a lower band in gold. Most of the ivory thimbles made during the seventeenth and eighteenth centuries were made in Dieppe and sent to Paris to be sold. And most of the gold, silver and silver gilt thimbles made in France during that time came from the town of Blois, on the river Loire. But thimbles were made in silver and gold in practically all countries, including Italy, Germany, Spain and Holland, where, at the end of the seventeenth century, one silversmith, Nicolaas Benschoten, built up a reputation for silver thimbles. If the French were the only ones to have made thimbles in coconut wood, the British seem to have been the only ones to make them in that typically British alloy, pinchbeck.

Most types of thimble, cheap as well as expensive, were made during the eighteenth century just as they had been in earlier times, but one kind emerged then that could not have been made in previous centuries, as Europeans did not know how to make porcelain. It is an amazing fact that the Chinese, who exported millions of pieces of porcelain to Europe through the various East India companies or 'compagnies des Indes', as they were known, never exported a single porcelain thimble; nobody has ever found a 'compagnie des Indes' thimble.

The European porcelain thimbles which were made during the second half of the eighteenth century are among the prettiest and most sought after by collectors who can afford them, for they always fetch high prices, especially if they are marked. Meissen, the well known firm in Saxony, was the main producer of porcelain thimbles; theirs are often decorated with one band, or with one or two very tiny panels edged in gold and containing little scenes. Others, probably made for the Dutch market, have figures and Dutch ships between the two bands. Many Meissen thimbles are decorated with seascapes, hunting scenes, birds or flowers. Many carry mottoes and inscriptions, always in French. One particular one, with a single band, has a cherry tree and a butterfly painted on it, with the inscription: 'L'amitié me garde' (Friendship keeps me safe). Another,

44

with a large single lower band, an indented higher band and smooth top, is painted with two cherubs holding a heart and bears the inscription: 'Mon feu durera toujours' (My love will last for ever). A rather unusual one is painted with two figures from the Italian *commedia del 'arte* and bears the motto 'Fidélité toujours' (Always faithful).

But Meissen, whose porcelain thimbles reach very high prices in salerooms and antique shops, was not the only factory to have produced them. Venice too made some beautiful examples in the eighteenth century: some with a single lower band painted with flowers, another with painted tulips and the motto: 'Avec le temps' (With time). The famous Du Pasquier factory was founded in Vienna in 1718 by a Dutchman, Claude Innocent du Pasquier, who in 1744 offered it to the Austrian government. While Meissen used the crossed swords as a trade-mark, the Du Pasquier factory used the Austrian shield. Du Pasquier thimbles are rarer than the Meissen ones, but as a rule the quality of their hard-paste porcelain is just as good. Most of them are decorated with flowers, some with scenes in cartouches, some with seascapes such as ships entering harbour. Meissen was the only firm to produce thimbles decorated with Chinese motifs, in the height of fashion in the last quarter of the eighteenth century.

The Chelsea factory produced thimbles which are very difficult to find today, even if one is willing to pay a high price. Starting in 1745, this factory, the earliest one in Britain, produced some of the finest and most significant soft-paste porcelain in England during the eighteenth century. It was established by a Huguenot, Charles Gouyn, and a Belgian goldsmith from Liège, Nicolas

Three nineteenth century thimbles. *Left to right:* Brass, with unusual indentations; brass, with a band of painted porcelain; ivory, from China. *Courtesy of the Kay Shuttleworth Collection Trust*

Chinese ivory thimble, circa 1850.

Sprimont, and most people in Britain have heard of its marks: the triangle, the raised anchor, the red and gold anchor. The factory was finally sold in 1770, with its contents, to the owners of the Derby factory.

One such thimble in a Paris collection, has an indented top and is painted with two gold-edged cartouches encircling a rose on a pink background. It is thought that the Derby and Worcester factories also produced thimbles during the eighteenth century. Following a fashion which started a few years ago when collectors were looking for porcelain thimbles, Worcester is today manufacturing some very attractive ones, but of course they have the drawback of not being old. The present Worcester thimbles are in hard-paste porcelain, painted with birds, flowers and fruit. A very few thimbles were made by the famous Sèvres factory in France, but most of the French ones were made by the numerous porcelain factories that sprang up in Paris during the second half of the century; many of these Parisian thimbles were in the Sèvres style.

Porcelain thimbles have always been more decorative than functional, although some people still think they were quite useful as they never caught delicate material such as silk. Good English examples were produced by the Minton and Rockingham factories. There are some beautiful, rare, eighteenth-century enamelled thimbles, and the Battersea factory, which lasted only a few years, is said to have made some of them. It is most likely, however, that they were made not in Battersea but in Bilston and other production centres in Staffordshire.

The nineteenth century produced a great variety of thimbles in all types of materials—brass, wood, copper, tin-plate, silver-plate, porcelain, pottery, tortoiseshell, ivory and even vegetable ivory (a tropical wood). Gold thimbles continued to be made, for some rich women insisted on them, not because the metal was valuable, but because it was clean and never become oxydized. Silver thimbles, with all kinds of decoration, were very common throughout the century, for they could be made with a very small amount of silver and therefore never cost much more than any other type. Some of them still carried the odd message inscribed on their sides, and some were decorated round the lower edge with tiny semi-precious stones like turquoise. Thimbles in filigree silver started to be made at the beginning of the nineteenth century by the Birmingham toymakers, who became known as 'wireworkers'. Other silver thimbles of the period, such as the Scottish ones, were decorated on the top with semi-precious stones like lapis lazuli, chalcedony, amethyst, rose quartz, cornelian and cairngorm. The tops of some silver thimbles were made of steel—a very good idea, for silver is a rather soft metal, and steel is much more resistant. In fact the majority of nineteenth century thimbles were made of steel. They were utilitarian and very cheap, and lasted a lifetime.

Wooden thimbles were made all over Europe, some of them banded in gold. They were made in bog-oak in Ireland, Germany and Austria; and elsewhere in sandalwood. Most French wooden thimbles were made in boxwood, and often delicately carved, but it has never been possible to trace the place of origin of these charming little thimbles. Yet other thimbles were made of tortoiseshell, a few being decorated with a band of gold. And there were some interesting glass thimbles, more decorative than utilitarian, that would grace any collection. Originating from an idea of eighteenth-century Venetian glassblowers, glass thimbles never really caught on. Collectors should have more luck, though, in finding examples of another type of thimble—the souvenir or commemorative thimble. For the Victorian period produced thimbles to mark certain occasions such as the Jubilee of Queen Victoria. And each souvenir thimble is a little conversation piece; most recently, souvenir thimbles in porcelain were made to celebrate the visit of Pope John-Paul II to Britain in 1982. Souvenir thimbles, which have never fetched high prices in the salerooms, were very often decorated with relief-

Nineteenth century French brass thimble, decorated with the bust of Napoleon. *Courtesy of the Thimble Society of London*

47

moulded views of famous buildings. French thimbles show representations of the Eiffel Tower, Our Lady of Lourdes, the Mont Saint-Michel in Normandy, Sister Theresa of Lisieux and other similar subjects. There was a time when one could find souvenir thimbles in practically every town, every seaside resort, every historic place. The vogue for souvenir thimbles spread all over Europe, as they were cheap and simple gifts that anyone could afford. A few were made of silver, but most were made of cheap metal, silver-plate, pottery, or porcelain. Souvenir thimbles represent good value for money, and they always look very nice in a collection.

The Japanese exported to Europe thimbles of ivory and bone, but it seems that the Chinese, who were very familiar with the thimble, never sent any to Europe. A great Parisian collector was lately complaining about this, for he has the most beautiful examples in his possession but not a single one from China. There is another rare kind of thimble of the period—rare because they had absolutely no value when they were made and would therefore have been thrown away by their owners within a short time. These were the ones that were given as advertisements for certain products; it was an ingenious idea, for the thimble, if used with a minimum of care, can last for a very long time—and so did the publicity on them.

Thimbles made of vegetable ivory are rarer today than the real ivory ones; many horn thimbles were produced during the mid-nineteenth century, but there is nothing very remarkable about them. Much more interesting is the double thimble, which as a rule is in silver, with an extra thick top that lifts off to show a glass cover under which could be inserted the portrait of a lover, for instance. Some mother-of-pearl thimbles were imported into Britain from France, and some glass thimbles were imported, this time not from Venice—although the Venetian glassblowers produced them

Matching thimble and finger guard in brown celluloid, early 1930s.

occasionally—but mainly from the many glasshouses of Bohemia. Then there are the thimbles that can be unscrewed to reveal a tiny perfume bottle, a miniature oil bottle or a very simple pincushion; some are even said to have concealed poison. The 'secret' thimbles of the period look exactly like ordinary thimbles, but halfway down, hardly noticeable, there is a groove which allows the top to be lifted off revealing a kind of secret compartment or hollow. There is absolutely no end to the variety of nineteenth-century thimbles, and to catalogue them all would be an impossible task.

From the end of the last century up to the First World War, some of the most marvellous thimbles were made by Russian silversmiths and goldsmiths, the most important being the famous Carl Fabergé, already mentioned, jeweller to the Imperial Court of Russia. Fabergé and other Russian thimbles were often of silver decorated with enamel in the old Russian style, making them more decorative than useful. Carl Fabergé also made thimbles in gold and silver, inlaid with semi-precious stones. And he made thimble-holders to match them.

Tiny silver sewing kit from Ypres, used by British soldiers during the First World War. *Courtesy of the Thimble Society of London*

More than any other needlework tool, the little thimble has made rapid strides in the collectors' world. More and more people everywhere, in Britain as well as on the Continent, are keenly collecting them. But, as usually happens when a specific piece starts to be collected, prices have risen during the last few years. With an eye to the future, some people are only collecting new thimbles, and some factories, as we have seen, have begun to produce them specifically for the collectors' market. They are found everywhere, perhaps in too large numbers, as the trend takes hold. The porcelain ones are made in Britain, France and Germany, very often decorated with flowers. There are also new ones decorated from top to edge in enamel, which look very pretty indeed, and silver ones. Once again, the only trouble with these charming little thimbles is the fact that they are new, and real collectors are only looking for antiques—which can still be found if one looks hard enough.

While collecting thimbles, one might as well look for finger-guards. The thimble protects the finger that pushes the needle through the material, but the needle passing through the material sometimes catches the first finger of the left hand. So someone invented the finger-guard, usually made in leather in earlier times. It was worn on the first finger of the left hand, the cloth being held between the first finger and the thumb. It thus protected the finger from the point of the needle. Some silver finger-guards were produced during Victorian times, but they are very rare.

Thimble-holders

Being very small objects, thimbles always had a tendency to disappear and to hide in the most unexpected places. The most elaborate and valuable deserved to be kept safely in special holders, so thimblemakers had the bright idea of selling their wares enveloped in little holders, made of all kinds of material and sometimes matching the object they were protecting.

Thimbles of the Middle Ages and the Renaissance are practically impossible to find on today's market. Some of them must have been kept in holders which are today even rarer than the thimbles themselves. Contemporary documents, which contain many references to thimbles, totally fail to describe the thimble-holders of long ago. They simply state, now and then, that a certain thimble was in a box or an *étui*—which is very frustrating. However, everything points to the fact that thimble-holders were already being made in France at least as early as the sixteenth century. Thimble-holders are mentioned in French wills and inventories such as that of the King of Navarre, already mentioned, in which one entry reads: 'a little casket in black leather containing two gold sewing thimbles, decorated with rubies'. And the King of Navarre, who became Henry IV of France, was not the only one to own such an object. As the entry reveals, thimble-holders then took the form of a casket covered with leather, and this type continued to be made until the

Rare and beautiful silver thimble holder, circa 1720. *Courtesy of the Kay Shuttleworth Collection Trust*

nineteenth century. Even in the sixteenth century thimble-holders were already made in the shape of the thimble they contained. The leather covering the holder was either black, red or green. The casket- or thimble-shaped holder was only one type among many others. In the eighteenth century thimble-holders were more common than in earlier times, and many beautiful casket-shaped ones were made of gold, silver, mother-of-pearl, ivory, leather or shagreen. Here, once again, the town of Dieppe produced some fine ivory thimble-holders.

Thimble-holders became very common in the nineteenth century, and were made all over the world in a great variety of shapes and materials. It is possible to find them today made of horn, ivory, polished wood, scented wood, porcelain, tortoiseshell, shagreen, leather, gold and silver. Some are the traditional casket-shaped container with hinged lid, the casket itself being covered with tooled leather (the usual material), and others are in velvet of various colours. Thimble-holders can be found in the shape of an egg or a barrel which could be unscrewed to reveal the thimble. For those who are not happy with the egg- or barrel-shaped holder, there are others in the form of a beehive. Wooden holders were made in all kinds of wood during the nineteenth century: they were always of the screw type, and in the form of acorns, urns, little turrets, top-hats, egg-cups and even pineapples. A favourite shape of the period was the nut-shell, the two halves being connected by a hinge. Some rarer thimble-holders are in the form of little wickerwork baskets. Some particularly beautiful ones were made of papier-mâché, which is perhaps not surprising since many workboxes and worktables were also made in that material.

But it is souvenir ware that offers the collector the greatest scope of all, and quite a lot of holders were made in Tunbridge Wells, Mauchline and Spa souvenir ware. The Scottish thimble-holders are most often made in the shape of a little knife-box covered with tartan or in sycamore wood decorated with transfers. The Tunbridge Wells thimble-holders are in the well known wood mosaic (see Chapter 8). Mauchline sycamore boxes and thimble-holders can be found on the continent, where they remain anonymous as few, it seems, in continental countries have ever heard of Mauchline. Similarly, hardly anybody has heard of Spa woods in Britain, and many lovely

Three silver thimbles made by Kay Thetford Kendall, a talented English sculptress specializing in bronze animals. Modern. *Courtesy of the Thimble Society of London*

boxes made in Spa and bought by British tourists in former times have been taken back to Belgium in recent years by Belgian tourists visiting Britain. Spa produced thimble-holders during the second half of the eighteenth century and throughout the nineteenth, all of them decorated with flowers on backgrounds of different colours, and heavily varnished. They fell within the cheaper range of objects sold in Spa shops. Another type found in the souvenir range is the egg-shaped thimble-holder, the most common of them all. These can be found in Tunbridge ware, in Mauchline ware and in Spa ware.

Since thimbles in filigree silver were made in Birmingham during the first half of the nineteenth century, it was quite logical for matching holders to be made in the same style. These silver holders seem to be quite rare nowadays. It is reported that thimble-holders were also made in gold during the last century—rich owners of gold thimbles must sometimes have wished to own a matching holder—but they must have been quite rare.

Exceptional jewelled thimbles were made in Russia during the last half of the nineteenth century by some of the most successful jewellers and goldsmiths from Moscow and St Petersburg, including, of course, Fabergé himself. Most of the thimbles being in silver or gilt, most of the holders are in silver, often decorated with enamel in the old Russian style. Gold thimble-holders were made in the last century by goldsmiths as important as Fabergé in Russia and Cartier in Paris. Such holders and matching thimbles would be worth a small fortune today. As all collectors know, holders are somewhat rarer than thimbles, as most thimbles were and still are sold as single items. But any of the holders would be well worth collecting.

When, around the turn of the century, the thimble started to show a lack of imagination in its design, thimble-cases followed suit. And the thimble became just what it was supposed to be originally: a utilitarian sewing tool, with no need for a special case.

Two wooden thimble cases, the one on the left having an embroidered 'strawberry' pincushion attached to it. *Courtesy of the Kay Shuttleworth Collection Trust*

4   SCISSORS AND SCISSOR-HOLDERS

Scissors

The English word 'scissors' and the French word *ciseaux* have the same meaning and both derive from the same Latin word *caesum*, 'cut', later confused with the Latin *scindere*, also to cut. Strange as it may seem, the Italians use the word *forbici*, which, clearly, does not have the same Latin root. The origin of scissors is very ancient, although scissors did not always exist in the form that we know them today. There are two types of scissors extant, one quite ancient, the other invented during the Middle Ages. The first of these cutting instruments were the spring scissors, called *forces* in French, or *forcettes* in the case of small ones. Spring scissors were made of two cutting blades without an axis to unite them, as in modern scissors, but with a half-circle acting as spring. These early spring scissors were used for a very long time by the fleecers of woollen cloth, by shearers to clip the wool off their sheep, and by stable grooms to trim their horses' manes. The other instrument, less ancient, is composed, as everyone knows, of two separate cutting blades held together by a rivet acting as axis, each blade ending in a ring to hold the thumb and the index finger.

Representations of the first type of scissors are found on ancient Christian monuments as well as on epitaphs of barbers, and a few have been found in tombs dating from the Dark Ages, including a fine example now in the Breslau Museum which was discovered in excavations in Sackrau, Silesia. The small spring scissors were used for centuries by tailors, seamstresses and housewives alike, well into the seventeenth century. Their existence is proved by numerous mentions in wills and inventories written as early as the thirteenth century.

Forcettes, or small spring scissors, are reported in the will of

Medieval scissors, circa 1400, a shape typical of this period.

Clemence of Hungary, written in 1356. The will of the French King Charles V (1338–80) indicates that he had in his possession 'a pair of small spring scissors in an *étui*'. In the long inventory (written in 1380) of the Château of Vincennes, near Paris, where Charles V was born and died, it is reported that there were 'des forcettes d'or à manches d'ybenus esmaillées' (a pair of spring scissors in gold with enamelled ebony handles), and others such as 'forcettes serrés de roziers enlevez'. It is a pity that the clerk who wrote the entry did not bother to give more complete details on the decoration of these spring scissors, for the expression 'de roziers enlevez' has no meaning today, although we know it refers to the decoration. In 1422, on the death of King Charles VI, another inventory was drawn up of everything in the Château of Vincennes, and one entry mentions 'des petites forcettes émaillées aux armes de France, de la reine Jehanne de Bourbon' (little spring scissors decorated in enamel with the arms of France, belonging to Queen Jehanne of Bourbon [the wife of Charles V]).

These few examples, chosen from many available, demonstrate that spring scissors were in use amongst the nobility during the Middle Ages. From the thirteenth century onwards, spring scissors were lavishly decorated with enamel, pearls and diamonds, and particularly with damascene (gold or silver inlay on steel). They were very often in gold or silver, and sold in protective holders, some of tooled leather and others of gold or silver. These splendid old scissors, very difficult to get hold of today, were quite exceptional and very different from those used by the common people—by the craftsmen of the Middle Ages, the tailors, the embroiderers and seamstresses. Unlike the rich, who bought their scissors from jewellers, they bought theirs from the mercers, a very important professional group in all European countries during the Middle Ages. The mercers sold simple, undecorated, spring scissors made of iron or brass. Many guilds, including the drapers' and the fleecers', bore spring scissors on their coats of arms. In fact the drapers of Paris were known as 'drapers of the big spring scissors'. In the fourteenth century the powerful guild of drapers in the town of Bruges, in Flanders, also sported a pair of spring scissors on their coat of arms. For many years no distinction was made in old texts between spring scissors and scissors as we know them today: both were referred to as *forcettes*.

For a long time it was believed in Britain and elsewhere that the scissors with two separate cutting blades joined by a rivet had been invented by the Venetians, in the sixteenth century. In fact, the antecedents of our modern scissors are much older. The scissors made in the Venice workshops during the sixteenth century were indeed famous all over Europe, for Venetians made vast quantities and exported them everywhere. But they never claimed to have invented them. And other Italian towns competed fiercely with Venice in the manufacture of scissors; many beautiful pairs used in Western Europe during the period were made in Milan, Padua or Naples. It was during the sixteenth century that the use of 'modern' scissors became popular, and they slowly replaced the old spring type.

In the marvellous twelfth-century stained-glass windows of Chartres Cathedral in France, one can still see, among various instruments of torture, an instrument which looks exactly like a pair of riveted scissors. Victor Gay, writing in the nineteenth century in his monumental work on the archaeology of the Middle Ages, mentions that he only managed to discover two representations of riveted scissors in documents dating from the beginning of the fourteenth century. One is a neat drawing of a pair of falconry scissors in a manuscript in the Richelieu Library in Paris, and the other is in a manuscript in the Besançon Library. Gay also states that the most ancient representation of a pair of scissors is in a Latin Bible of the tenth century, but unfortunately he fails to give the source

Above: Very long iron scissors, probably of Spanish origin, early seventeenth century. *Below:* Large iron scissors with handles in the form of chimeras and an Arabic inscription on the lower parts of the blades. Mid fifteenth century. *Courtesy of Ader Picard Tajan, Paris*

A collection of unusual scissors. *Top:* Sixteenth century Persian iron scissors in the form of a sacred bird, its wings studded with turquoise. *Centre, left to right:* A seventeenth century Indian bethel cutter in the shape of a woman; seventeenth century European steel scissors, the handles shaped like boars; An Indian bethel cutter in the form of a dragon (seventeenth century). *Bottom, left to right:* Turkish iron scissors of the eighteenth century, showing traces of gilding; seventeenth century Indian scissors in iron. *Courtesy of Ader Picard Tajan, Paris*

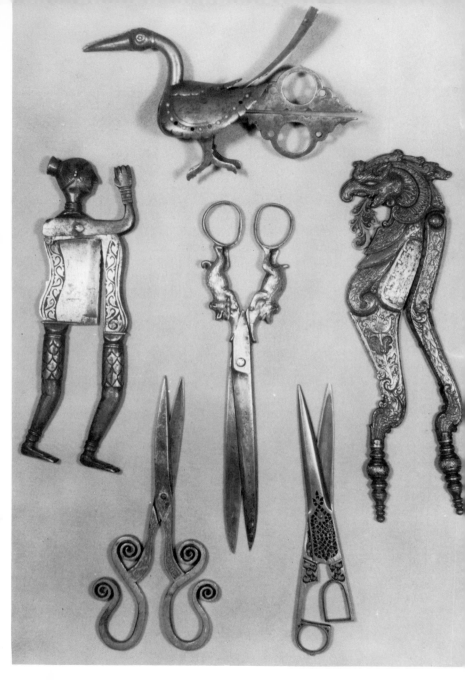

56

of the information. And many mediaeval texts mention *ciseaux* (scissors) as opposed to *forcettes* (spring scissors). In the famous *Roman de Renard*, written about the year 1200, one can still read:

> Ciseaux bien tranchants et basin
> Et un rasoir bon et fin
> (Good cutting scissors and a cloth
> And a good, fine razor)

If the anonymous writer of the *Roman de Renard* could mention scissors so casually in the year 1200 or thereabouts, it can only be because they were already quite common and had probably been so for some time. To go back to Clemence of Hungary, whose inventory was full of surprises even in 1328 when it was written, one entry refers to 'three pairs of scissors'. And in the well known inventory of Charles V, so often a subject of study, one finds 'unes petites cisailles d'or toutes plaines' (a small pair of scissors, in plain gold). In the inventory of Charles VI written in the year of his death (1422), we find that he owned 'deux cisailles d'argent dorées de la forge de Clermond, dont les bouts des manches sont en 2 cc et endroit le clan d'une couronne' (two pairs of scissors in gilded silver from the Clermond forge, the handles ending in two Cs and decorated with a crown). (That the handles were shaped like two Cs seems the most likely interpretation.)

There are many references to scissors in mediaeval documents, and as we have already mentioned, scissors were represented on the coats of arms of various guilds. So the old assertion that the

Three pairs of steel seventeenth century scissors, the top one probably of Spanish origin, the other two, decorated with damascene, of Islamic origin. *Courtesy of Ader Picard Tajan, Paris*

A very elaborate pair of Spanish scissors in steel inlaid with brass, made in Andalusia in the seventeenth century. *Courtesy of the Victoria and Albert Museum*

Venetians invented them in the sixteenth century is, clearly, unfounded. From the fifteenth century onwards, references become more and more numerous. As we have seen, riveted scissors appear alongside spring scissors in the 1422 inventory of Charles VI. Even earlier, in 1401, in the inventory of the possessions of the Queen of France, we find an even more detailed description: 'A Guillaume Turel, varlet de la garde-robe de la Reyne, pour l'argent que lad. dame lui a donné pour avoir siseaulx de Toulouse à tailler les garne-ments de lad. dame' (To Guillaume Turel, keeper of the Queen's wardrobe, for the money given to him by the said lady, for scissors from Toulouse made to cut the Queen's clothes). In 1412, a few years later, we find representations of riveted scissors on the plaque out-side the dressmakers' guild in Paris. The plaque, usually in brass, depicted the professional tools of the various guilds.

An entry in the accounts of King Louis XI, dated 1471, reads: 'A Olivier le Mauvais, varlet de chambre et barbier du Roy, la somme de 2l et 12s pour l'achapt et le paiement d'un estuy garnys de rasouers, cyseaulx, forcètes, peignes et autres choses servant à son métier, le tout garny d'argent' (To Olivier the Bad, valet and barber to the king, the sum of 2l and 12s (2 livres and 12 sols) for buying and paying for an *étui* containing razors, riveted scissors, spring scissors, combs and other things needed in his profession, all decorated with silver). A document of 1560 in the French national archives reads: 'For a pair of scissors from Moulins, contained in an *étui* of tooled leather, to clip the nails of the said milord [the King])'. And the accounts of 1590 of the 'small pleasures of the king' records: 'To Guillaume Cassin, for a barber's *étui* in silver gilt containing six razors with handles in silver gilt and two scissors in gilt'.

From the last few references we learn that in the Middle Ages at least two French towns, Moulins and Toulouse, were known for the manufacture of scissors. But they were not the only towns to share that reputation, for Italian towns like Milan, Padua, Venice and Naples were already much more famous than the French centres. In the sixteenth century scissors were manufactured on a large scale in Italy, Spain (mainly in the town of Cordoba) and France, and also in the Middle East in countries like Persia and Turkey, which exported large quantities of scissors to the West. These oriental scissors were often copied in the Western world, particularly the Persian ones featuring a bird, with its beak forming the two blades. The Victorians copied this type of scissors, which were very popular then. Other oriental scissors of the time were made so that they seemed to have only one blade and one functional finger ring, the second ring being placed above the first as an ornament.

Some European scissors, from the sixteenth century onwards, were also quite attractive. A well known French pair, for instance, featured a pageboy with rounded shoes constituting the rings, with his hands holding two plumes which in fact were the cutting blades. One also finds scissors in the shape of a harlequin juggling with two hoops formed by snakes biting their tails. The most famous pair produced during the eighteenth century was the *jambes-princesses*, scissors in the form of booted legs (constituting the two blades plus their handles). As early as the sixteenth century, even some scissors made for the ordinary people were decorated with gold, damascene and engraving. And from the seventeenth century, scissors were often engraved with emblems, intertwined hands, hearts surmounted by a flame or with love inscriptions. The Sauvageot collection in the Louvre contains a pair of seventeenth century scissors engraved with the inscription 'Je me fie à vous' (In you I trust). The fashion of offering scissors and other sewing tools to young brides, begun in the sixteenth century, would last until well into the nineteenth. For women could never manage without scissors in their household, and well-wishers always saw to it that they received some on their wedding day. Many scissors were engraved with the coat of arms of the owner — which gave them a special personal quality. Even the divine Madame de Pompadour, the mistress

German scissors from the end of the nineteenth century, decorated with portraits of Kaiser Wilhelm II and his wife.

of Louis XV to whom Lazare Duvaux supplied many a beautiful pair, including 'une paire de ciseaux de Berge, damasquiné en or' (a pair of scissors from Berge with gold damascene), needed scissors. Berge was a very well known Parisian jeweller of the time. In the archives of the Duvaux firm there are also references to other pairs of scissors sold to the extravagant Pompadour, such as 'five pairs of scissors made to cut tapestries', and 'two pairs of scissors for the toilette'.

Many beautiful plain scissors were produced during the eighteenth century, very similar to those already produced a hundred years earlier. But a new type came into being at this time—folding scissors, invented apparently by a certain M. Chomète who had a workshop in the Place Dauphine in Paris. The invention is claimed by the French in all contemporary documents; it was quite an innovation, as these new scissors did not need an *étui* and could safely be kept in one's pocket. Folding scissors were produced in quantity mainly during the nineteenth century, and in fact they have been made right up until the present day. But can the claim that Chomète invented them be substantiated? For Savary des Bruslons, writing at the end of the seventeenth century, comments: 'One appreciates very much the *little pocket scissors* from Châtellerault, Moulins, Nevers and Toury, but they cannot be compared with those made in Paris, which are of great beauty and sold at an extravagant price.' Which little pocket scissors was Savary talking about? They might have been folding scissors, easy to keep in one's pocket.

England was not slow to establish her own scissor trade, and by the eighteenth century the English manufacturers were considered as good as any. Like those of Paris and other capitals, London toymakers of the time sold scissors in luxurious *étuis* or small cases of filigree silver, shagreen, enamel, leather or pinchbeck, although some especially fine scissors inlaid with mother-of-pearl were still imported from France. In England the production of scissors was centred on the town of Sheffield, where the trade had been started at the end of the eighteenth century by a Robert Hinchliffe who made scissors in crucible steel. As usual, it was not long before

Pair of Napoleon III silver scissors, decorated in the style of the Louis XVI period.

Birmingham discovered that the scissor trade was a lucrative one. Solingen in Germany followed the British examples and, together with Sheffield, has remained the main centre of scissor production until today.

Some collectors claim that antique scissors are harder than ever to find, and it is certainly true that you need a fair amount of luck to discover old iron scissors, sixteenth-century scissors from Persia and Turkey, from Venice, Milan or Naples, seventeenth-century scissors from Moulins, Châtellerault or Toury — and many other kinds. It seems that even the more unusual nineteenth-century scissors are difficult to find, as in many countries they have already been collected. A strange state of affairs, considering that millions of scissors, in strong metals and therefore not perishable, were made in Sheffield, Birmingham, Solingen and other towns throughout the last century. It is still possible, now and then, to come upon a good nineteenth-century pair with handles in mother-of-pearl, usually still in their *nécessaire*. But where are all the buttonhole scissors, made in the last century, mainly by Walker and Hall of Sheffield? These can easily be identified from the regular gap in the blade and the screw between the two parts which was used to alter the size of the hole being made. Even the stork-design scissors, copied from the well known sixteenth-century Persian scissors, are not always very easy to find either. And these continued to be made throughout the Victorian era, mostly in steel, some partly gilt.

Scissor-holders

At least from the fourteenth century onwards, scissors were often kept in special holders, which were usually made of plain leather. A pair of scissors might not have been sold in a holder, but owners soon realized the danger of carrying them attached to their belts or in a pocket.

Mediaeval holders may not have been particularly striking, but in the sixteenth century they began to be more luxurious, for the women who wore them suspended from their belts wanted them to match the splendour of their dresses. Men as well as women used scissors, not only to clip their nails with but also to open their letters, which were then closed with ribbons and sealed with wax. There are many documents that demonstrate that scissor-holders were sometimes lavishly decorated. In 1538, King François I of France, who had expensive tastes as everyone knows, bought from the goldsmith Jehan Cousin of Paris an *étui* which contained a pair of scissors and other tools. The *étui* was in ebony, containing a comb, a mirror, a pair of scissors and a brush to clean the comb, all decorated with gold damascene and set with rubies and turquoises'. In the inventory of Gabrielle d'Estrée, the mistress of Henry IV, there is a reference to her owning 'deux étuis à mettre ciseaux garni l'un de diamants, l'autre de rubis et de diamants' (two gold *étuis* for keeping scissors, one decorated with diamonds, the other with diamonds and rubies). In the same inventory, we find another scissor-holder covered with embroidered black velvet. This type of scissor-holder, often made of cardboard covered with velvet of various colours and embroidered with gold and silver thread, remained fashionable throughout the seventeenth century.

In both the seventeenth and eighteenth centuries scissor-holders were not always of the expensive kind, as one might well have imagined, but were commonly made of engraved or openwork iron, and sometimes of iron decorated with damascene. Even these rather crude holders were inscribed with gallant mottoes. *Etuis* for scissors remained fashionable throughout the eighteenth century, as most of the noble ladies had nothing better to do than to spend their time in embroidery and other needlework; even Madame de Pompadour, who was a very busy woman, bought many beautiful pairs of scissors from her usual supplier, the well known dealer Duvaux, who sold her scissors and scissor-holders of the most expensive kind. (He also sold them to Marie-Antoinette.) For a perfect

Seventeenth century Dutch scissors case in enamelled gold.
Courtesy of the Victoria and Albert Museum

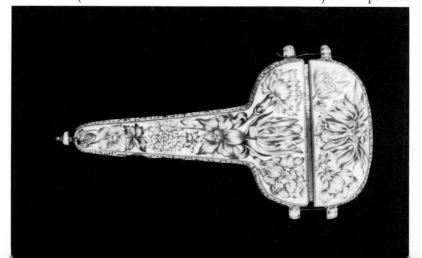

fit, scissor-holders were made to measure—in tooled leather, in damascene silver to match the scissors, in chiselled or engraved silver, in openwork steel or in brass. In England many beautiful scissor-holders were made in pinchbeck. And both in England and in France they were also made—like everything else—in shagreen. The Duchess of Brissac always kept her scissors in 'un étui de roussette verte' (an *étui* of green shagreen).

Shagreen, as we said earlier, was called by the French *peau de chagrin, peau de roussette* or *galucha(t)*. It was not always made from shark's skin, however, but sometimes from the leather of wild asses from Persia and Turkey; the town of Tauris, in Persia, was the main Middle-Eastern production centre.

Shagreen-covered holders were very popular in France and England during the second half of the eighteenth century. It was about that time that porcelain scissor-holders began to appear, but only a small quantity seems to have been produced, as porcelain was really much too fragile for the purpose. Meissen in Saxony, the makers of some of the most beautiful porcelain thimbles, also put onto the market some of the prettiest scissor-holders one could wish to own. They were made to fit the scissors that were sold with them, and had a cover with a silver hinge. The holder was decorated with figures inspired by painters such as Watteau, Boucher and Fragonard, some in full colour, others in red or blue monochrome. Although scissor-holders have always been available, most scissors were kept in *étuis* containing other sewing tools or toilet accessories.

At the end of the eighteenth century *étuis* were also made in steel decorated with cut facets, a fashion that persisted during the first twenty or thirty years of the nineteenth. In a French women's magazine called the *Journal des dames et des modes*, dated 25th June, 1819, we read: 'the little ladies have, to keep their scissors, holders made of sandalwood decorated with cut steel facets. These holders are flat or spiral-shaped.' The writer adds that other sewing-holders were in machine-turned wood, very finely worked and decorated with a multitude of cut steel facets.

The nineteenth century saw the gradual decline of scissor-holders, but they never quite disappeared completely. Today they are still being made in leather or in plastic, but collectors are not interested in modern items—for modern items have no soul.

Beautiful old scissors and cases. *Top, left to right:* sixteenth century iron case; gold-mounted scissors in a gold case ornamented with medallions on a blue background (eighteenth century); gold-mounted scissors in silver enamelled case inscribed 'Souvenir d'amitié', French, eighteenth century. *Below, left to right:* scissors in chased silver case with châtelaine attachment, seventeenth century; silver-mounted scissors in seventeenth century green enamelled case; gold-mounted scissors in unusual eighteenth century gold case. *Courtesy of Ader Picard Tajan, Paris*

5 CHÂTELAINES, NÉCESSAIRES AND WORKBOXES

Châtelaines

From the early Middle Ages until the nineteenth century it was the custom for the lady of the house to carry a clip or similar device on her belt to which she could attach her keys, scissors, spoon, knife, bodkin, *étui*, needle-case and whatever else she pleased. Some women of long ago must have worn very heavy belts indeed.

At the beginning of the eighteenth century the belt clip was replaced by a *châtelaine*, a French word which, literally translated, means 'lady of the castle'. And the *châtelaine* must indeed have been, at least at the beginning, the property of the lady of the castle, hence this most appropriate term for a novel object consisting of a hook-plate to which were attached small chains, from which, in their turn, various items could hang. Any small object could be attached to a *châtelaine*—such as watches, keys, knives—but a lot of them only carried sewing tools like scissors in scissor-holders, needle-cases and thimble-holders, some of which contained thread.

The *châtelaine* probably appeared first in France, and most of the surviving examples are dated after 1740, although some beautiful *châtelaines* in gold had already been produced during George II's reign, in about 1720. The form of the *châtelaine* hardly changed from the moment it first appeared until it went out of fashion during the last century. Some were quite simple, but others, of the luxury type, were very elaborate, with a series of small lavishly decorated panels chained together. Beautiful, now very rare, gold *châtelaines* were produced in England, France and Switzerland between 1760 and 1780. Very few gold ones were made in England, for most of them were made in that strictly British alloy, pinchbeck. Here not only the *châtelaine* was made in pinchbeck, but all the other items suspended from it—the scissors in their cases, needle-cases and

Châtelaine featuring Wedgwood jasper cameos set in cut steel, probably made by Matthew Boulton at his Soho works in Birmingham, circa 1785. The cameo at the top depicts Hygeia, Goddess of Medicine. *Courtesy of the Wedgwood Museum, Barlaston*

thimble-holders. Many *châtelaines* were made in the eighteenth century, with a pin-case and a thimble in an *étui*, of which there is a very good specimen in the Museum of London.

Many *châtelaines* made in France at this time were lavishly decorated with enamelled panels, some painted with flowers, others with typical eighteenth century scenes inspired by famous French painters of the time. Some are in gold, most in silver. But *châtelaines* were not only produced in precious metals which only the very rich could afford; they were also made in light steel from about the middle of the eighteenth century, when the steel works at Woodstock started making steel jewellery. Woodstock not only produced *châtelaines*; it also produced very elaborate scissors which were already in 1770 very expensive items—four or five times the price of ordinary pairs of scissors made anywhere else. The *châtelaines* from Woodstock had the usual hook-plate made of steel, to which were attached a number of chains composed of steel slivers or leaves. As usual with steel jewellery, the *châtelaines* were sometimes embellished with cut steel facets, and from them hung every kind of sewing tool—thimbles, scissors, needle-cases, even pincushions. The production of cut-steel jewellery continued well into the nineteenth century, in France as well as in Britain. Another type of cheap metal jewellery, known as 'Berlin iron jewellery', which began to be produced in Berlin around the year 1804, is similar in appearance to cut-steel jewellery, but *châtelaines* were never made in Berlin.

Birmingham, which became famous for its steel jewellery after the great industrialist Matthew Boulton started his factories in the Soho Works, also made delightful *châtelaines*, which at the time sold quite cheaply. In about 1773 Matthew Boulton started his well known association with Josiah Wedgwood, the great potter from Stoke-on-Trent, and from then on quite a lot of *châtelaines* were embellished with Wedgwood jasper ware cameos. British steel jewellery was very expensive on the Continent at the end of the eighteenth century, and Birmingham, Wolverhampton and Sheffield continued to export their wares in vast quantities all over the world. This time the French caught on very quickly and started making their own steel jewellery, including *châtelaines*. Once the intensive competition between French and British manufacturers had brought down prices, steel jewellery became popular and fashionable. Even the famous merchant, Grancher in his shop 'Au petit Dunkerque' in Paris, was selling all kinds of objects in steel during the last quarter of the eighteenth century—including *châtelaines*, ornate scissors of the Woodstock type, necklaces and brooches. In fact there was absolutely no difference between the British and the French products. Even the Wedgwood *châtelaines* cannot be attributed to one country rather than another, for Josiah Wedgwood, good businessman that he was, exported his cameos all over Europe, including France, where they could be mounted. And many continental porcelain factories in France and Germany copied the famous jasper ware. A *châtelaine* decorated with jasper ware cameos would have to be completely dismantled if one wanted to see the trade-marks at the back of the cameos. Without taking such drastic measures it would be impossible to attribute a *châtelaine* to Birmingham rather than to Paris. And, moreover, there would have been no way of telling whether Wedgwood cameos might not have been mounted in Paris.

About the middle of the nineteenth century, at least on the Continent, the *châtelaine* was replaced by yet another kind of sewing-tool container. It would take women a long time to stop hanging tools from their belts, a fashion that went back as far as the Middle Ages, and the *châtelaine* was replaced by a small leather bag that hung by two chains from a hook. A whole set of sewing tools including cylindrical pin- and needle-cases was provided inside the bag, to which could be added thread and any other small tools. Hence, at the end of the nineteenth century needlewomen could still carry everything they needed attached to their belts, just as their mediaeval predecessors had done.

Nécessaires

Thimbles, pins, needles, scissors, thread and other small but necessary sewing tools were sometimes assembled all together in one special container called a *nécessaire*.

In the eighteenth century there were all kinds of *nécessaires*, some large, others small enough to put into the pocket or handbag. The most important *nécessaire* was the toilet- or dressing-case, a big box containing many smaller boxes in which could be kept all the necessary personal items to do with washing, dressing and grooming. As bathrooms hardly existed at this time, travellers had to make do with a wash-basin in their bedrooms. So they had to take their combs, soaps, perfumes, brushes, earpicks and toothpicks with them in a dressing-case. Travellers would equip themselves not only with dressing-cases or *nécessaires*, but also with writing-cases, breakfast-cases and jewel-cases. Men had beautiful shaving *nécessaires* con-

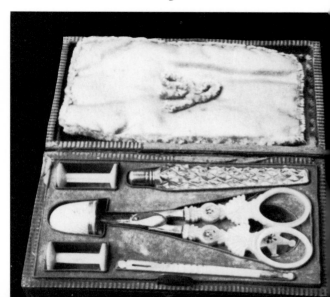

In its original box, this nineteenth century French nécessaire contains scissors and thimble in mother-of-pearl, a cut glass needle case with a silver top, two spools and an ivory tape needle. *Van Hove Collection, Brussels*

A beautiful workbox in wood covered with material, the inside of padded silk. *Folklore Museum, Tournai*

taining brush, soap, mirror and razor. One of the smallest *nécessaires* was the sewing kind, which contained all that was necessary for emergency repairs. It could be small enough to be suspended from a *châtelaine* or kept in a pocket.

The sewing *nécessaire* seems to have been already in fashion in the mid-eighteenth century, and it is still being made today. Early *nécessaires* could be very sumptuous indeed, judging by the various inventories still extant. In the inventory of the famous French painter Nicolas de Largillière, drawn up in 1756, there is a reference to a 'small *nécessaire* in filigree silver'. In a public sale in Paris that took place on the 6th October 1779 some beautiful *nécessaires* were sold; according to the catalogue, one of them was 'an attractive *nécessaire* in oriental agate, engraved and set with twenty diamonds, mounted on gold, with inside pieces in gold and other pieces mounted in gold.' We may not be too sure what the 'pieces' referred to were, but it gives some idea of how lavishly decorated were these *nécessaires*. The following entry in the same sales catalogue is more explicit, mentioning a 'pocket *nécessaire* in green shagreen, containing a pair of scissors, a mother-of-pearl-handled knife with a gold blade, a gold needle, one pencil and ivory tablets.'

Not all *nécessaires* of the period contained items of a single category, but a combination of sewing, dressing and writing tools. English *nécessaires*, like the French, came in various sizes and often contained different combinations of accessories; many were decorated, in the eighteenth-century fashion, with amateurish inscriptions in French, quite often misspelt. *Nécessaires* were probably to be found in England about the middle of the century; certainly by 1770 they were on sale in the London shops. At the same time in Paris, ornate *nécessaires* could be bought in all the fashionable shops, including 'Au petit Dunkerque', Grancher's shop, where queens, princesses and the entire French nobility used to get their trinkets. Even Marie-Antoinette could often be seen on the quai Conti, where the shop was located. And before her, Madame de Pompadour had spent a small fortune there. Grancher, jeweller to Marie-Antoinette, advertised all kinds of pocket *nécessaires* in shagreen and gold, in the January 1778 issue of the *Mercure*.

Nécessaires of all kinds were made during this period—in gold, silver, shagreen, tooled leather, and enamel on gold or silver, most of them cube-shaped. But the French Revolution put a stop to such extravagance, and for a long while the production of *nécessaires* in precious metals decorated with enamels or precious stones, as well as other expensive items, was discontinued.

But it was not by any means the end of the sewing *nécessaire*. The nineteenth century saw a proliferation, the most common of which consisted of a flat box in any one of a variety of shapes and sizes, in all kinds of materials, including wood, leather, mother-of-pearl and tortoiseshell. And although, unfortunately, the extraordinary extravagance of the eighteenth century was gone for ever, many *nécessaires* were lavishly equipped with beautiful items in mother-of-pearl, including scissors and thimbles. Little square *nécessaires* in mother-of-pearl were also produced from the beginning

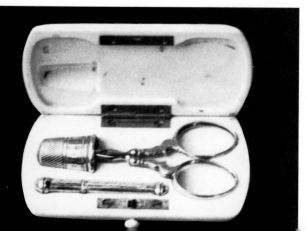

Small silver nécessaire in an ivory box, probably French nineteenth century. *Van Hove Collection, Brussels*

A nineteenth century nécessaire in leather.

of the nineteenth century; these contained what could be called emergency tools. The prettiest mother-of-pearl container, still much sought after by collectors and rather difficult to get hold of, was in the shape of an egg, which opened to reveal the sewing tools.

A very popular *nécessaire* of the period—and they were sold in practically all European countries—was the miniature grand piano fitted with a musical box and containing, under its cover, elaborate sewing tools. This model was made for decades and in large numbers, and still appears now and then in sales and in antique shops. Another *nécessaire*, in fact a small workbox, was the so-called 'lady's companion'; cube-shaped, usually in tooled leather, and containing a pair of scissors, a thimble, a needle-case and a few other items, it became popular in the nineteenth century, having first appeared during the last decade of the eighteenth. The *nécessaire* that most continental women chose to use during the second half of the nineteenth century was in the form of a tiny handbag, complete with handle and containing all kinds of sewing tools.

Workboxes

It is often thought that the workbox, fitted with compartments, wells and drawers and supplied with sewing tools, was first made in the middle of the eighteenth century, and that the oldest were in Chinese lacquer and imported from China at the end of the century. These lovely workboxes were indeed fitted with delicately carved ivory silk-winders and spools, but they were certainly not the first to be seen or used in Europe; workboxes were made here long before the Chinese thought about them. In fact it is probable that the idea was suggested to them by Europeans trading in the Far East.

Europeans had always made all kinds of boxes, in every kind of material, to suit all kinds of purposes. Many lovely ones had been made as early as the Middle Ages, and long before the eighteenth century some of them must have been used to keep sewing implements. Sixteenth- and seventeenth-century boxes were usually square and made of oak sometimes carved, sometimes decorated with marquetry, encrusted with mother-of-pearl, or inlaid with brass or pewter wire. At the end of the seventeenth century, the usual oak was replaced in England by walnut, and boxes were also made with materials such as tortoiseshell and parchment. The most beautiful ones, made during the Stuart period and very rare today, were covered with stumpwork, a kind of embroidery in relief. Stumpwork, already produced during Queen Elizabeth's reign, took the form of needlework pictures, often representing biblical scenes and used to cover small cabinets, among other things. Stumpwork

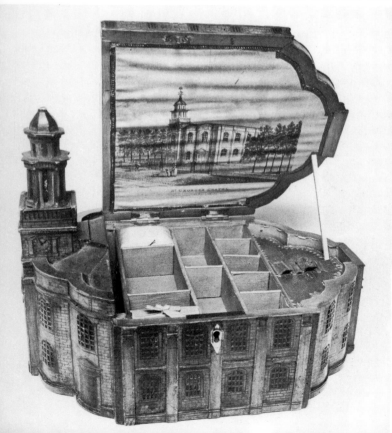

Rare workbox in the form of a church, believed to have been made in Great Yarmouth in 1819 by John Preston (1771–1855), for his wife who attended St George's Church there. *Courtesy of Great Yarmouth Museums' Elizabethan House*

boxes were already fitted with compartments and drawers, and it is most likely that women keen on needlework found them ideal for holding not only their cosmetics and jewels but also their sewing tools.

Specific references to workboxes are rather rare in contemporary documents, and even those that do exist are not detailed enough. In the inventory of Queen Marguerite of Austria, for instance, written in 1524, we find a reference to a box covered with green velvet containing 'une forcette, ung petit ciseau et dix autres petits instruments y servans ayant les manches d'escailles, de perle et le surplus dorez' (a pair of spring scissors, one pair of riveted scissors, and ten other small instruments with tortoiseshell, mother-of-pearl and gilt handles). Was this a workbox or a big *nécessaire*? The number of tools mentioned implies that the container must have been quite large.

Many wooden boxes were imported from South Germany into all European countries throughout the seventeenth century, and some shops sold nothing but boxes. The most specialized shop in Paris during the second half of the century was that of the widow Poisson, whose name has passed to posterity and who had a shop at the sign of the 'Pierre de lard', where she sold 'all kinds of boxes from Germany, in pine or other white wood, painted or unpainted'. Some of these German boxes were no doubt workboxes. Large and beautiful boxes, now rare, were produced in Spa at this time, some of them with compartments. They were made in plane wood, inlaid with scroll work composed of thin pewter and brass wires, painted with birds and flowers, the flower heads being of natural or stained mother-of-pearl. In the last decade of the century they were replaced by boxes in imitation Chinese lacquer, for which Spa became famous all over Europe. Some of these Spa lacquer boxes, with black, red, green or blue backgrounds and fitted with compartments, were particularly noteworthy; they were used as dressing-cases and workboxes, according to Spa Museum.

At the end of the seventeenth century, craftsmen from Normandy produced big wedding caskets, with hinged lids, carved in oak with roses, stars, and hearts pierced by arrows. Inside were small compartments and wells, and a drawer was fitted in the base. These workboxes were given to brides as a wedding present. Normandy also produced another type of workbox, also given at weddings, which came in three sizes and were decorated with charming naive paintings of flowers and birds on a green background. By the beginning of the next century workboxes were being made everywhere. In *Les amusements des eaux de Spa*, a book published by an anonymous author in 1735 and printed in Amsterdam, we read that among all the wooden trinkets to be found in the souvenir shops of Spa were 'lacquer boxes, walking sticks, *workboxes* and tea-boxes, liquor-boxes, brushes and many other little items, varnished and decorated with tender inscriptions or mottoes.' In 1762 a certain Doctor Limbourg published in Paris a book called *Les nouveaux amusements des eaux de Spa'*. In it he writes: 'We had already done some shopping, but nothing could prevent us buying a few more trinkets. So we bought *workboxes*, necklaces, ear-rings and bracelets'.

Many of these Spa workboxes can still be seen in collections and in the charming little Spa Museum. Workboxes continued to be made and used throughout the eighteenth century, and it was only during the last two decades that Chinese lacquer workboxes started to appear everywhere. But the nineteenth century was the century of the workbox, and indeed of boxes in general, for there is no end to the variety of boxes made during Victorian times. All kinds of special-purpose boxes were produced—picnic-boxes, shaving-boxes, jewel-boxes, game-boxes, writing boxes, paint-boxes, smoker's boxes, pharmacy boxes. They were made in all kinds of woods, decorated with marquetry or ormolu, or inlaid with mother-of-pearl; and they were made in tortoiseshell, bone and papier mâché. The more popular kinds continued to be made for decades, as did the souvenir workboxes from Spa, Tunbridge Wells, Sorrento and Scotland. The most common workbox of the Victorian era was the simple wickerwork box with silk or satin lining. Another type, thought to have first appeared at the end of the eighteenth century and in common use by about 1820, was the double-lidded workbox in wood, painted and decorated with scenes or flowers, sometimes engraved, and fitted with a handle for carrying it around the house. The double-lidded basket continued to be made until well into the twentieth century.

The miniature chest of drawers was also a well known type of workbox, fitted with a compartment just under the lid, and the drawers below enclosed by a pair of doors or a hinged flap. Some of these delightful chests of drawers were made during the Regency period in mahogany or rosewood. Quite a few were made a little later in papier mâché, rather heavily decorated with mother-of-pearl or painted with scenes or flowers in cartouches, sometimes with a large pincushion inside the lid. The miniature grand piano type, fitted with a musical box, does not belong to the workbox category as it was only a sewing *nécessaire*, like the small workbox called the 'lady's companion'.

There are some very interesting workboxes, difficult to get hold of, that were made by French prisoners of war in England between 1756 and 1815, the year of the Battle of Waterloo. Two prisons were built especially for them—the Norman Cross Prison in Peterborough and the Princetown Prison on Dartmoor—and they were also held in other jails in England, Scotland and Ireland. To make a little money, they made all kinds of trinkets that they subsequently sold or exchanged with the local people. Some, who had been cabinet-makers, knew how to carve. Ivory not being available, they carved bones they could get from the prison kitchens. Others knew the technique of straw work, a craft that was popular on the Continent but less so in England. With odds and ends, pieces or wood, bones, bits of ivory and straw, they produced little masterpieces: model ships, model guillotines, mechanical toys and domino boxes, but also needle-cases, thimbles and thimble-cases, lace bobbins and workboxes. Their bone workboxes, like their model ships, are today very much sought after by collectors and museums. Their bone workboxes may be the most beautiful, but they also made some very interesting ones in straw work.

Beautiful workboxes have, of course been propuded in papier

A workbox in straw work, made by French prisoners of war circa 1800.
Courtesy of the Victoria and Albert Museum

75

mâché, mainly in England but also in France. Pretty but fragile, these boxes were called simply 'papier mâché workboxes' in England, while the French called them 'Napoléon III workboxes'. Most of the French workboxes of this style were made of pearwood painted black. French workboxes in other woods were decorated exactly like the British papier mâché boxes, and it is difficult from a distance to differentiate between the two. Both were over-decorated, in colours that were rather too bright, and painted with the same sort of scenes in the usual cartouches. Both were decorated with mother-of-pearl inlays.

The French have always claimed to have invented the technique of papier mâché. And it may be true; already in the royal accounts of 1562 there may be a reference to papier mâché. One of the entries reads: 'A Charles Padouan, mouleur en bassetaille, le somme de L livres pour plusieurs testes de mousles, feuillages, de corniches et figures de bassetaille de papier pilé couvert de poiraisins et d'autres étoffes' (To Charles Padouan, mould-maker, the sum of £50 for several moulds, foliages, corniches and other figures in *crushed*

English papier maché workbox, decorated with painted ornament on a black background, circa 1840. *Courtesy of the Victoria and Albert Museum*

paper, covered with *poiraisins* [probably a kind of pitch resin]).
Many papier mâché objects seem to have been made in France during
the eighteenth century; the famous jeweller Grancher advertised
in the August 1775 issue of the *Mercure* his 'plateaux et autres ouvrages en papier mâché, avec peintures étrusques d'après la publication
des antiques du chevalier G.Hamilton' (trays and other works in
papier mâché, painted with Etruscan scenes taken from the engravings of artefacts published by Sir G.Hamilton). It may well be that,
since the material is always called in England by its French name,
papier mâché, the French did indeed invent it.

A certain Watson had the idea of setting up a papier mâché business in Birmingham; he was followed soon after, in 1772, by another
Birmingham man called Henry Clay, an expert in japanned work
who made his own kind of papier mâché, with excellent heat-
resisting qualities. He first produced trays, then varnished panels
for coaches, and all kinds of cabinets, tables, worktables and workboxes. In 1802 Clay moved to Covent Garden in London, where he
was to remain very active for the next fourteen years until, in 1816,
Jennes and Betteridge took over his business. Around 1825 the new
firm introduced mother-of-pearl decoration into all kinds of items—
cabinets, chiffoniers, beds, cradles, pianos, as well as worktables
and workboxes—exhibiting them in the 1851 Exhibition. Pearl
decoration on papier mâché was used until the 1850s. Although the
last manufacturer did not close down until 1920, the papier mâché
business was all but finished by the last quarter of the nineteenth
century. All kinds of cheap imitation papier mâché workboxes were
made, but they are not to be compared with the most beautiful and
sought after specimens made by Clay and Jennes and Betteridge.
French papier mâché workboxes, of which very few were made,
are of a poorer quality than the British ones.

Workboxes have continued to be made right up to the present
day. A design that was very popular on the Continent from the 1920s
onwards was a box with six compartments, three on each side,
hinged one on top of the other, which could be opened outwards
rather like two vertical accordions. The same model fitted on legs
became a popular worktable. Workboxes like this are still being
made in wood today, although cheaper models in plastic are also
available.

6 WORKTABLES

Many people collect workboxes, but few collect worktables, although most of them would grace any living-room. Unfortunately antique worktables tend to command high prices in all countries— not only the beautiful eighteenth-century ones but even some of the best ones produced during the nineteenth century. And they are not plentiful either.

Worktables started to be made in France during the second half of the eighteenth century. Nobody has ever discovered one made before 1750, and it seems that before then nobody ever thought about making a special table, with drawers, compartments and wells, in which rich women could keep their sewing equipment. Now they could sit at their worktables embroidering, sewing or making tapestries, without ever having to move an inch to get the tools they wanted. First to have the idea of worktables were the great cabinetmakers who worked in Paris during Louis XV's reign— craftsmen like Bernard Van Riesenburgh, Jean-Henri Riesener, Van der Cruise-Lacroix and a few others who designed furniture for the Palace of Versailles, masterpieces in the Louis XV style, made with expensive woods like rosewood, violet wood and lemon wood. During the second half of the century they made all kinds of small tables, light and easy to move around, for all kinds of purposes.

There has always been some confusion about the correct names for these tables. At the time, the French solved the problem by calling them all 'ladies' tables', whatever they were for. All, with a few rare exceptions like the shaving table, were made for women. Even the Parisian merchant Lazare Duvaux, main purveyor of small tables (and other very costly objects) to the ladies of the French court of Versailles, called them 'ladies' tables', without ever, apparently, thinking to differentiate between them. Vast numbers of small tables were made by the great cabinet-makers of the century, though not by ordinary carpenters, who were not allowed to work with precious woods or to do marquetry. These cabinetmakers made thousands of writing-tables, dressing-tables, *tables à transformations* combining several functions in one table, and shaving tables. They also made *chiffonnières*, sewing tables, *tricoteuses* and other worktables, including 'drum tables' (*tables tambours*). The tables could be round, oval, kidney-shaped or rectangular, with three legs or four, and always very elegant, with their tops in marquetry or marble encircled by a brass rail, and compartments under the flaps if they had flap tops, or with small drawers if the top was rigid.

The *chiffonnière* was a very small table with a rigid top, equipped

Probably the most valuable worktable in the world, made, circa 1785, for Queen Marie Antoinette by Martin Carlin (Master 1766) and J. Pafrat who probably finished it after Carlin's death in 1785. It is of marquetry, ornamented with gilt brass and Sèvres painted porcelain. The lower drum, on fluted legs, has a divided lid opened by a spring. In 1786 Marie Antoinette gave it to a Mrs Eden, later Lady Auckland. *Courtesy of the Victoria and Albert Museum*

Combined work and gaming table in rosewood with brass mounts and inlay. English, circa 1830. *Courtesy of the Victoria and Albert Museum*

with three drawers, two at the front and one at the side, the front drawers usually being hidden by a little door. Like all Parisian furniture of the Louis XV style, they were lavishly decorated with ormolu mounts. Sometimes the *chiffonnière* was fitted with a shelf between the legs. Some *chiffonnières* had a kidney-shaped top, always in marquetry or marble with the usual brass rail, except at the front, where there were three tiny drawers hidden by a door. In some rarer cases they were fitted with two pivoting compartments, one on each side. Others were oval, still with three little drawers.

The Louis XV *table tambour* (drum table), which was nothing like the British drum table, was one of the nicest small tables ever made. It had a round top, usually in marble, marquetry or even hand-painted porcelain, encircled, except at the front, with a brass rail about one inch high. The drum table had only three legs, with or without a shelf, and the drum itself was fitted with three tiny drawers. Some very expensive and luxurious worktables were made by L.Boudin, master cabinetmaker in 1761, and by the three Bernard Van Riesenburghs (father, son and grandson) who made beautiful tables—sometimes in marquetry, sometimes in imitation Chinese lacquer, with porcelain tops. Pierre Migeon, merchant and cabinet-maker to Madame de Pompadour, has always been considered the great specialist in small tables. Jean-François Oeben, supplier to Lazare Duvaux, who himself supplied Madame de Pompadour, made the masterpiece known as the 'king's desk', now at Versailles. He also made some exquisite worktables, one of which was sold in London in 1960. It was a small, round table with three levels and with three legs, all in flower marquetry, with the top encircled by the usual rail. The flap top revealed a workbox. Roger Van der Cruise (called Lacroix in France), master cabinetmaker in 1755, made some remarkable worktables, including one in *vernis Martin* with a yellow background and a top in Sèvres porcelain. The top has a bronze rim, and the shelf between the four legs is encircled by a brass rail. He made others, some in the drum style, in marquetry and in *vernis Martin*, but his masterpiece is the table described above, now in

Worktable made in 1760 by P. Garnier and J. P. Ledoux of France, of ebony and mahogany marquetry with gilt brass mounts and an inset plaque of soft paste Sèvres porcelain. *Courtesy of the Victoria and Albert Museum*

81

the Nissim de Camondo Museum in Paris. The same cabinetmaker also made *tables à transformations* which could be used as a dressing-table, writing-table or worktable. The rectangular table top is decorated with flower marquetry, with a rail all round except at the front. There is a narrow drawer under the top fitted with a flap mirror, and two deeper drawers on each side.

The fashion of making small tables, including worktables, continued during the Louis XVI period, although furniture of the style to which it gave its name was made a good fifteen years before Louis XVI came to the throne. After the heyday of Versailles was over, the nobility started to move back to their country estates. People wanted rather more simple furniture; Herculaneum had not long before been excavated, and they began to look to the styles of the classical world for their inspiration. The Louis XVI style was indeed simpler, but in appearance only. In fact it was still very far from real simplicity, and classical styles were interpreted liberally.

Tables continued to be made in lacquer, mahogany, marquetry and painted wood. Worktables were found, square, rectangular or oval, the great change being in the legs which, having been curved, became straight. For the first time, some Louis XVI tables were mounted on castors. Worktables, sewing-tables, drum tables and *chiffonnières* remained more or less the same, except for the legs and for the fact that for some reason round tables ceased to be produced. Instead of being supported by four legs, worktables were more often than not supported by two lyre-shaped struts. A good example of this kind was a new worktable that appeared at the end of Louis XVI's reign, the *tricoteuse*, especially for women who indulged in knitting. The top was a deep tray, supported by the two lyre-shapes, with a second tray underneath. The front of the top tray, which was attached by two hinges, could be lowered. This type of work-table was also made by Riesener, and one of the finest examples of his work is the *tricoteuse* he made for Marie-Antoinette which is now in the Château of Fontainebleau. Made about 1785, in extra-ordinary mother-of-pearl marquetry, it was decorated with ormolu and polished steel mounts. The Louis XVI cabinetmakers also invented yet another worktable, the *table à ouvrages-liseuse*, which could be used for reading and for sewing. It was composed of two round trays, edged with brass rails, on a central tripod leg. The top tray was fitted with a double-branched candlestick.

But not all French worktables of the eighteenth century were made by the Parisian cabinetmakers; some very nice examples, albeit in plain wood, were produced by the carpenters of Paris and of the provinces. Some carpenters made delightful little worktables with rectangular tops, with two or three drawers underneath on four cabriole legs. They showed perhaps more imagination in certain provinces—some experts now believe that the real birthplace of the worktable was Anjou where, very early in the century, they made oval worktables supported by two plain, solid wood sides joined by an open compartment where the sewing tools were kept. Be that as it may, most of the provincial worktables one comes across today date from the nineteenth century. And one of the best examples is the *guéridon de veillée*. *Veillée* is a difficult word to translate into English: it conveys a gathering of people who would meet in the evenings to engage in some mutually agreeable pursuit. A special table was made in the province of Auvergne for lacemakers and needlewomen, to use during their *veillées*. The table top was in the form of a round tray supported by a central tripod, with a second tray placed at a lower level. The women used to sit around it, and five clear glass bottles filled with water would be placed on the top tray round a central candle, an effective way of diffusing the light. On the second, lower tray all the sewing or lacemaking tools were put. One can find in Provence yet another type of worktable, a very simple one, consisting of a casket supported by four, generally straight, legs. A pincushion was fitted inside the flap top, and a lower shelf was intended for the workbasket and sewing tools.

In eastern France, mainly around the town of Lyon, they produced a very extraordinary worktable which is not found anywhere else. It is a very elaborate affair consisting of a central leg supported by a tray on three short splayed legs. The top of the table is a kind of round box, edged with a sausage-like pincushion, and the box

Drawings of two nineteenth century French provincial worktables. The lower one, from Auvergne, stands on tripod feet and has two trays, one rounded and the other square. The one above is typical of the Lyon region, its top comprising a deep tray surrounded by a circular pincushion, with a small drawer underneath. The height of the upper part is adjustable. *Document ABC Decor, Paris*

itself is supported by four short spindle-legs, with a drawer underneath it.

Sheraton, one of the great designers of his time, designed quite a number of fragile ladies' tables, with ingenious arrangements of drawers and sliding tops. Like their French counterparts they were meant to be moved from room to room, so they were made light and delicate. It was Sheraton who popularized the Pembroke table, which had semi-circular flaps attached to a rectangular centre, and tapering legs. But even though women must have used the Pembroke table for sewing, it has never been a real worktable. Some Sheraton-style worktables were mounted on four tapered legs or on trestle feet, with sometimes just a drawer and a pouch to hold the needlework and other sewing implements. Another type of Sheraton worktable was the so-called 'French worktable', consisting of a tray on trestle feet with a shelf below.

During the Regency period all kinds of tables were made for all kinds of purposes, among them some beautiful worktables. Following the French idea of *tables à transformations*, the cabinetmakers of the time produced a table for playing chess and backgammon, combined with a lady's workbox and a writing surface. In fact, whatever sedentary household occupation you might be engaged in, you could use this table. It was practical, light and easy to use. Many of these all-purpose tables were fitted with a pouch or a silk bag under the top. Quite a few of them were supported, in Louis XVI style, by sides in the form of lyres. Now, unfortunately, they are very rare.

Regency cabinetmakers used rosewood, kingwood (a beautiful Brazilian wood) and zebra-wood (the striped wood of the Guiana

French Charles X work-writing table in clear maple wood with amaranth inlay, supported by two lyres. *Courtesy of Ader Picard Tajan, Paris*

84

tree). Many rosewood worktables were inlaid with brass, with tops in the form of a casket on any of a variety of legs. One interesting contemporary model stands on a pedestal base, with a coloured silk pouch underneath the top. It is fitted with a games board which slides from under the oblong table top, and there is also a square centre section lined with leather, with a backgammon board underneath. Below it there is a removable sliding chessboard above a workpouch, and on each side two d-shaped compartments with lids. None of these multipurpose Regency tables is exactly beautiful, but they were probably the most useful tables one could find in a household.

From the end of the Louis XVI period, but mainly during the Empire, the French made furniture in metals such as green bronze, gold bronze, wrought iron and even steel, including small tables for lunches *à l'anglaise* and various kinds of worktables. The Empire worktable in metal has a round top on a central pedestal and three baluster legs resting on a thick triangular base with in-curving sides. The three legs can be in the form of the various types of sphinxes described in Egyptian and Greek mythology, monopteral lions, or the hind legs of felines. Guillaume Janneau, ex-director of the Mobilier National in Paris, states that the triangular base of tea- and worktables was often decorated with an incense-burner. Other Empire worktables—round, square or rectangular like the *tricoteuse*—were made in various kinds of wood and always decorated in characteristic Empire style.

Biedermeier worktables

Some of the most beautiful worktables, complete with all the necessary sewing tools, were made not in England or in France but in Austria and southern Germany. The French always gave the names of their kings to their various furniture styles; the English gave them the names of their great cabinetmakers and designers. The Austro-Germans gave to the style that flourished at the beginning of the nineteenth century the name of a person who did not exist—Biedermeier.

The origin of this name has been the subject of much speculation.

Beautiful French Louis XV worktable attributed to the famous cabinetmaker J. F. Oeben, decorated with floral marquetry and ormolu mounts. *Courtesy of the Victoria and Albert Museum*

One line of thinking is that it was the product of the imagination of a lawyer from the Baden region, based on the common expression for a decent German bourgeois—*Bieder Bürger*. From there it was tempting to replace the word *bürger* by Meier, a name as popular in Germany as Smith in England or Dupont in France. But some authors maintain that Biedermeier is in fact the amalgam of the names of two German comic characters, Biedermann and Bummelmeier, and the *New Columbia Encyclopaedia* states that it is now believed to derive from the name of the worthy, bourgeois-minded Papa Biedermeier, a character featured in a series of verses by a certain Ludwig Eichrodt. It is all very puzzling, but whatever the true explanation, the fact remains that Biedermeier is a fictional character symbolic of all the bourgeois-minded citizens of southern Germany and Austria immediately after the Napoleonic Wars.

The style in question covers more or less the period between the Battle of Waterloo in 1815 and the Revolution of 1848. In 1815 Vienna was the artistic centre of Europe. The Austrians who remembered the French occupation of their country no longer wanted to import furniture from Paris or to copy French styles. They wanted to be themselves, and as they were in a homely mood and no longer cared for foreign wood like mahogany, they started using their own wood – walnut, maple, wild cherry and ash – which were lighter than mahogany. The Viennese did not care any more for elaborate ornaments, either; they wanted something gay, simple and, preferably, cheap. So they invented the Biedermeier style. Thousands of delightful worktables were made, complete with needlework tools hidden under flap tops. The Biedermeier style is whimsical, with a touch of baroque. It can be amusing, even ugly.

One beautiful specimen is in the Victoria and Albert Museum, London. It is veneered with very light-coloured woods and has kept all its original sewing equipment. It is rectangular and on four curved legs, with a flap top fitted inside with a mirror. Another Biedermeier specimen, now in the Schleswig-Holstein Museum, is rather like a drum table on two lyre legs resting on a thick round base. The lyre legs are, of course, very neoclassical, but the general shape of the table is unmistakably Biedermeier.

Restoration and Louis-Philippe worktables

The beginning of the Biedermeier period in Austria corresponded more or less with the beginning of the Restoration period in France. This style, which lasted until about 1830, was a reaction against the pageantry and extravagance of the First Empire. The French, like the Austrians, decided that mahogany was too heavy and reverted to their own kinds of wood. And instead of making heavy furniture with stout bronze mounts, they made delicate, light pieces in wood often inlaid with brass wire, which could be found anywhere in the country. Restoration furniture is simple and elegant, and its decoration is always discreet. Quite a lot of worktables were made in the new style, particularly round, oval or rectangular ones. They are always in the form of a workbox supported on two s- or lyre-shaped struts. The flap top of the workbox lifts to reveal an interior with various compartments on one or two levels; the inside of the top is graced with a mirror or, more often, with a large pincushion. To make it even more useful, there is a wide gutter between the two supporting sides, to hold tools and other sewing materials.

Many more worktables were also made in the style that came next, the Louis-Philippe style, which covers roughly the period between 1830 and 1848. A comfortable style like its predecessor, Louis-Philippe is a bit heavier than the Restoration style and often shows mediaeval, Renaissance and Louis XVI influences. But now production had become mechanized, which explains why so many worktables of this style are extant. The cabinetmakers of the time started making wooden furniture painted black and with painted decoration, already heralding the Napoleon III style. In order to keep their furniture very simple, they did not use heavy ornaments or bronze mounts. It was a bourgeois style made for the bourgeoisie.

Like her predecessors, no lady of the Louis-Philippe period could manage without the help of a worktable, and some very interesting ones were produced. The most popular type consists of a rectangular top on four console legs, joined together by an oval shelf or a single straight crossbar. Once again the hinged top can be lifted to reveal wells and compartments. The prettiest and rarest of Louis-Philippe worktables was also rectangular, with a top composed of two flaps opening outwards, revealing yet another flap fitted with a mirror. Under it was a well, equipped with variously sized compartments to hold the tools. The whole was supported by four baluster legs on castors, and in between the four legs there was a deep drawer which could be pulled out. These worktables could be found in any kind of wood, for the cabinetmakers of the period used mahogany, violet wood, ebony, yew, beech, sycamore, lemon tree wood and maple, the light wood being used mainly for lining.

Napoleon III and English papier mâché worktables

A new furniture style developed in France after the 1848 Revolution: it was known as the Napoleon III Second Empire style. A composite style which flourished from 1848 until about the fall of the Empire in 1870, it produced a lot of very nice pieces of furniture which were more or less copies of Louis XV and Louis XVI specimens. Many copies in the even older Boulle style were also made. Quite a few, now very expensive, worktables were made in that particular fragile style, decorated with inlays of brass, pewter and tortoiseshell.

The Napoleon III style took definite form when cabinetmakers started making furniture in the English fashion, with exactly the same type of decorations as in England—black backgrounds painted with scenes, flowers and birds and inlaid with mother-of-pearl. But whereas in England this type of furniture was made of papier mâché, in France it was made of wood, usually pear wood. Only a very few worktables in papier mâché were made in France. Many kinds of worktables can be found, even today, in that charming Napoleon III style. Some of them are in the form of a workbox supported by four baluster legs joined together by two bars, usually with a pouch hanging from the box top. Others are workboxes supported by a single central pedestal on a tripod; these are similar to the papier mâché worktables made in England during the same period, and it is impossible to determine which side of the Channel introduced that particular type of decoration, with the black background painted with flowers and birds, gilding and mother-of-pearl inlays. Also, it can be hard to tell the difference between an English papier mâché worktable and a Napoleon III specimen. The French ones are most often in wood, which is indistinguishable, at a distance, from papier mâché. And to confuse the issue more, producers of papier mâché furniture like Jennes and Betteridge also made tables in wood, and a lot of their mountings were in wood, too.

These fragile pieces, both French and English, faded out in the 1860s, although some later examples, usually of inferior quality, are still to be found. Napoleon III worktables could be bought very easily on the Continent up to about ten years ago, but now they are becoming rather rare and the prices of good quality specimens have soared. Both types are so fragile that collectors must be warned that only examples in perfect condition should be bought, as they are practically impossible to restore—so fragile, in fact, that the least error in handling, even spilled water, will harm them irreparably.

Art Nouveau worktables

All kinds of worktables of no particular style were made throughout the nineteenth century, most of them in the form of a workbox supported by a central leg. The last worktables of a recognizable style were those produced during the Art Nouveau period, from 1890 until the beginning of the First World War. Not many were made, so they are nowadays valuable collectors' pieces. Most have a top supported by four very sinuous legs or two sides carved from one piece of wood. Underneath the top, between the legs, they are fitted with an intermediate shelf, sometimes with a rim round it. The legs are joined by a crossbar, usually well carved. Few worktables of this period are known to exist, and one would have to have real collector's luck to discover one. The Art Nouveau worktables were not the last to be produced, but all the rest are less old and cannot be considered as antiques. All the same, they could well become the antiques of the future. That is the way great collections are sometimes made, and it is the cheapest way.

7   SEWING MACHINES

Sewing machines are not often collected by ordinary collectors of sewing tools, but museums are now very interested in them—as well they should be, for the sewing machine revolutionized the art of sewing during the second half of the nineteenth century. It was an invention that the entire world found invaluable. Before the sewing machine, making clothes took up a lot of women's time. Women who could not afford help had to make all the family's garments by hand—the children's dresses and underwear, and the husband's shirts, underwear and work clothing, as well as their own clothes. There was no end to what had to be sewn. So the invention of the sewing machine proved to be as important to mankind as the electric light bulb, radio and television, and the automobile.

But no single person could claim to be the inventor of the sewing machine. For it was invented by many people, just as the aeroplane was, and it reached perfection via many ideas, improvements, patents, lawsuits, trials and defeats. The construction of an efficiently working model belongs to the nineteenth century, but the idea of building a machine capable of replacing the hands of a seamstress was already in the air at the end of the previous century. Many men thought about it, dreamed about it, but the main mistake at the beginning was to attempt to devise a machine which would imitate ordinary hand-sewing. Many tried and many failed. One of the first to try was an Englishman called Thomas Saint, who as early as 1790 patented a crude stitching device that was never successful. In fact, nobody knew about it until nearly a hundred years later when the patent was discovered in the cupboards of the British Patent Office. In his request for a patent, Thomas Saint described a 'quilting, stitching and sewing machine for making shoes and other articles.' Did Saint ever build his machine? No one knows, but a replica of it exists in the Thimonnier Museum in Lyon. Others tried

Left: A reconstruction of the Thomas Saint sewing machine of 1790, built according to the specifications of his patent. *Right:* The world's first sewing machine, invented and built by the Frenchman Thimonnier in 1830. *Thimonnier Museum, Lyon*

towards the end of the eighteenth century, but their initial efforts were fruitless, once again because they usually tried to copy the motions of hand-sewing.

Between 1790 and 1830 many people racked their brains over the problem, obtaining patents for sewing devices but never managing to build a prototype which could really sew. Inventors still had not thought of using a needle with a hole near the point, and their cloth still had to be fed through by hand. Then the Americans moved onto the scene. The French and, of course, the Americans agree that the nearest to a workable sewing machine was concocted in 1804 by two Americans, Thomas Stone and James Henderson. Their machine was a very primitive affair, not at all practical and producing poor results.

Then came the machine invented by a poor Frenchman called Barthélémy Thimonnier, a tailor who was born in the village of Arbresle in the Rhône département in 1793, but who had moved to the village of Amplepuis where he was to die in 1857. There Thimonnier devised a sewing machine that would really work. By 1825 he had managed to build a working model, a very clumsy affair made mainly of wood, and in 1830 he took out a patent for it. It looked nothing like a modern sewing machine, but it worked, and it could reproduce a kind of chain-stitch. (With the chain-stitch machine, the needle throws the thread out in a loop under the material. The next stitch then throws a loop through the first loop and the stitches on one side become a chain.) Thimonnier took out patents for various improvements in 1845 and 1848. The machine caused its inventor a lot of problems and never brought him much money. He took his improved model to Paris, where some eighty copies were built to be installed in a workshop located in the rue de Sèvres, where uniforms for the French Army were being made. Thimonnier became the supervisor. But, as happened so many times during the Industrial Revolution, workers became frightened. Their great fear was of becoming unemployed and facing starvation, as a result of the introduction of the machines. One night a mob attacked the Paris workshop and destroyed the whole establishment. The disappointed

The Bekh sewing machine has been in the same family since 1863, still in its original box and with its instruction booklet.

Thimonnier returned home. His machine was exhibited at the Great Exhibition of 1851; one of them is in the Thimonnier Museum in Lyon and another in the Arts et Métiers museum in Paris, but one would be most unlikely today to find another Thimonnier sewing machine.

Before his death Thimonnier patented two new improvements and even obtained patents of further improvements in Britain. But in 1848 there was a revolution in France, and people had other things on their minds than sewing machines. Even in Britain there was a total lack of interest, and when the Thimonnier machine was exhibited in London in 1851 it completely failed to attract the attention of the public. The Thimonnier chain-stitch machine had no bobbin and only one thread.

While the Thimonnier sewing machine was having its ups and downs in Europe, the Americans had entered the arena for good, and many improvements were to come from the United States. In Britain in 1841, Archibald and Newton had patented not a sewing machine but a very important item, a needle with an eye near the point, often known as the eye-pointed needle. But they had been preceded in America by a New York Quaker genius, Walter Hunt, who had devised a lock-stitch machine between 1832 and 1834. Hunt knew nothing about Thimonnier and had never heard of Archibald and Newton. He had the idea of using an eye-pointed needle and managed to build a lock-stitch machine using two threads instead of one, one passing through a curved eye-pointed needle and the other coming from a shuttle. The two threads locked tightly after each stitch, hence the name. But he was not so keen on his machine once his daughter told him that it would throw seamstresses out of work. He applied for a patent in 1852, but his claim was refused as such a machine had already been patented in 1846 and the eye-pointed needle in 1841.

Although it was he who had first had the idea of the lock-stitch, Hunt was too slow. For another American, Elias Howe Jr., a Cambridge (Massachusetts) machinist and a man of great foresight, had come in on the act. It was not until 1843 that he turned his attention to sewing devices, but by 1844 he had completed a rough model and by 1846 had obtained a patent for it—the first patent for a lockstitch machine. Where Hunt had been slow, Howe had moved very quickly. For at first, like so many other unsuccessful inventors, he had attempted to reproduce hand-sewing, but after studying weaving he realized his mistake and adopted the shuttle, the double thread, and the eye-pointed needle invented by Walter Hunt. The Howe machine sewed straight seams a few inches at a time. The material was fastened to a small metal plate a few inches long and fed into the machine vertically. It was not very practical, for if the material was longer than the plate it had to be refastened to it.

The Howe machine was sold to an Englishman, William F. Thomas, for £250. Thomas, a corset manufacturer, secured the British patent in his own name, but had the decency to engage Elias Howe to work for him on a weekly wage. Howe, discontented and still poor as a church mouse, went back to the USA in 1849. Back home he discovered that inventors had been very busy in his absence and that many of them were infringing on his rights. Numerous machines had been built around the middle of the century, the most important being the Lerow and Blodget which had a curved shuttle, adjustable feed and automatic tension. And the year Howe arrived home, John Bachelder had patented the very first sewing machine to employ the horizontal table with a continuous feeding device capable of sewing any length of material. Even two years earlier, Allen B. Wilson of Michigan had built a very crude sewing machine which, nonetheless, worked perfectly well. The Wilson machine was of the lock-stitch type, the lower thread being carried by a double-ended shuttle, and it was the first one to be equipped with an automatic feeding device. It could sew curved seams and even turn a right angle, which no previous machine had been able to do. It became known as the 'two-motion feed', but the inventive Wilson soon devised a 'four-motion feed' which he patented in 1854. A lot of other inventors were hard at work too in the early 1850s, and among so many who were infring-

Left: A quite rare American sewing machine by Wilcox & Gibbs, circa 1860. *Courtesy of the Great Yarmouth Museums' Elizabethan House*

95

ing on poor Howe's patent rights was the most notorious of them all, Isaac Merritt Singer, who patented his first sewing machine in Boston in 1851. In Singer's machine the material was not hung on a plate like so many others, but rested on a horizontal table and passed under a straight needle that worked vertically, as they still do today. Elias Howe started proceedings against all those who, he thought, were infringing on his rights—which brought him more money than he would have made if he had decided to build his own machines commercially.

In 1851 yet another two Americans, Grover and Baker, came out with yet another machine and more improvements. Their machine 'had a double loop stitch made by the combination of a circular reciprocating underneedle and a curved upper eye-pointed needle'. But the innovation of the Grover and Baker was that it could use threads from commercial spools. By 1856 there were three main American sewing machine firms: Wheeler and Wilson, Grover and Baker and, of course, Singer. Singer went on to found the world's best-known company, which still bears his name. Until the Singer, all machines were driven by a hand-turned wheel, but soon Singer added the treadle, which gave more power, permitted greater speed and left both the operator's hands free. The Grover and Baker machine was soon perfected by M. Goodwin.

In the second half of the century machines began to be manufactured everywhere—in Britain, Germany, France and particularly in the USA. Otys Avery made his first machine in 1852, the French firm Journaux-Leblanc, in France, in 1854. The three main American concerns, tired of all the legal proceedings imposed on them by Howe, formed a cartel agreeing with Howe to stop, once and for all, all litigation. The same year, a farmer from Virginia devised a chain-stitch machine which was soon improved by a certain James Wilcox from Philadelphia. It became known, the world over, as the Wilcox and Gibbs sewing machine. Thousands of patents were filed and issued in the USA and Europe. The manufacture of sewing machines became quite an industry on both sides of the Atlantic, the United States always being in the forefront, with forty-six different firms in 1914. The best-known machines that were on sale in Europe around 1875 were the Singer, the Wilson, the Wilcox and Gibbs, the Hurtu, Journaux-Leblanc and Hautin, the Grover

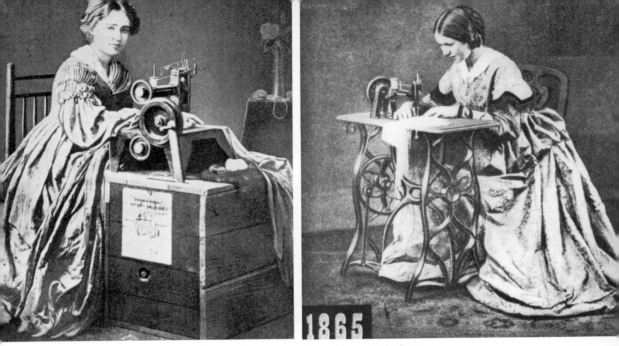

Early Singer sewing machines. *Left:* the first lock-stitch machine made by Isaac Merritt Singer in Boston in 1851. *Right:* The foot treadle machine of 1865. *Courtesy of the Singer Sewing Machine Company (UK)*

and Baker, the Rumpf, the Seeling, the Kayser Zig-Zag, the Lecat, the Pollach Schmidt, the Grollet and the Adam-Garein.

Statistics show that by 1873 about three hundred thousand sewing machines were sold each year in the United States, fifteen times more than in France. The prices of sewing machines were very high; an average sewing machine would cost some 225 francs in Paris, while the average worker earned one or two francs a day. So in Europe and in America sewing machines began to be paid for in instalments, the Singer firm being probably the foremost exponent of the new scheme. It was Edward Clark, Singer's partner, who seems to have fathered instalment selling. Singer was already branching out everywhere. Singer sewing machines were first manufactured in Clydebank, Scotland, in 1867. The assembly of Singers began in Montreal in 1873, and a large factory was opened the same year in Elizabeth Port, New Jersey. The very first Singer sewing machine (1851) was too heavy for domestic use, and the first Singer family sewing machine appeared in 1858. It was called the 'Grass-hopper' by the factory workers, but was commonly known as the 'Turtle Back'. But this machine was a little too light and another, which was to become famous, came out in 1859—the 'Letter A'.

Vast numbers of sewing machines were made during the nineteenth century and over five hundred different firms are known to have existed, each one with its own ideas about how the machine should work and look. Some very strange ones were made, too, some bow-shaped or circular, and other, much rarer ones in the form of horses, lions or squirrels. Many of these strange machines were made by firms that did not last long, and they are not at all easy to find. It is always fun for a collector of sewing items to discover one of those rare pieces that have not yet reached a high price on the market—machines with long-forgotten names such as Lecat, Journaux-Leblanc, Hurtu, Rumpf, Kayser, Grover and Baker, Anker, Junker Ruh, Muller, Jones, Taylor, Dorman, Adam-Garein, Moldacot, Gritzner and Seeling, and many others that are not even recorded. Antique sewing machines are not always big and clumsy, and they could well form part of a private collection. Many firms, particularly Singer, produced miniature machines that could be used by housewives as well as little girls. Sewing machines can be seen

An English sewing machine of 1873, made by Edward Ward and called 'Arm and Platform', in front of its original case. *Thimonnier Museum, Lyon*

A beautiful Pollach-Schmidt sewing machine, 'La Silencieuse', made in 1872. *Thimonnier Museum, Lyon*

in some museums, mainly folklore museums, but not in great numbers. To see large collections one has to go to Scotland or to France. One of the largest collections of vintage sewing machines is in the Clydebank Museum in the Clydebank Town Hall, Scotland, which has some five hundred machines on display, half of which are Singers. The other museum worth visiting is the Thimonnier Museum in Lyon, where the Thimonnier firm still survives.

8 SOUVENIR WARE SEWING TOOLS

Spa Ware

'Spa' is a word which is well known the world over, as it is the name given to a certain kind of health resort in Britain, the United States and Greece amongst other countries, but few people outside Belgium realize that the name has been borrowed from an actual town called Spa in eastern Belgium, which is the most ancient spring-water health resort in the world. People started going to Spa to drink its waters during the Middle Ages. The small town is located some fifteen miles east of Liège, capital of the Walloon country, and it has been for centuries the Mecca of European hypochondriacs. Kings, princes, dukes, great artists, scholars, politicians and musicians would meet in Spa to take its spring waters or to enjoy themselves. For Spa had the first organized legal casino in the world, opened in 1769. It also had the first racecourse on the Continent.

As well as many other achievements in the field of entertainment, Spa promoted the first souvenir ware industry in the world. The first Spa souvenirs were made in the second half of the sixteenth century, when people flocked to Spa to cure themselves of disease. News travelled fast even in those days, and the King of France, Henri IV, sent his own personal doctor to Spa to test those wonderful waters; Agostino, doctor of Henry VIII, was charged with the same mission. The town was not yet organized for receiving tourists, and visitors had to walk up and down the steep hills to reach the various springs. So the first objects sold in Spa shops were walking sticks, in plain natural wood at first. But once the local inhabitants had discovered that a painted stick was ten times more attractive than a plain one, sticks appeared for sale painted and decorated.

The carpenters and painters of Spa began to be interested in the souvenir business, and from the beginning of the seventeenth cen-

Beautiful eighteenth
century Spa workbox,
decorated with views
of Italy. *Spa Museum*

tury they made all kinds of objects for the visitors, such as boxes, caskets, bellows and dressing-cases. These souvenirs, probably the nicest ever made in the town, were painted with flowers, birds and fruit or inlaid with mother-of-pearl. The central cartouche, also in mother-of-pearl, was carved with various scenes and most of the boxes were also inlaid with thin brass or pewter wire.

In 1690 the style changed. Craftsmen started making boxes and other items in imitation Chinese lacquer; they became very good at it and their reputation spread all over Europe. A Doctor Edmond Nessel published a small book on Spa in 1699, in which he writes:

It is a real pleasure to see the thousands of *jolités* [Spa souvenirs] that the inhabitants of Spa sell to their foreign visitors, who never go home without buying a few of these locally made objects. These *jolités* are always in wood, varnished in the Indian manner, flat or in relief, gilded and highly polished. In Spa they use all kinds of paints, but also mother-of-pearl, tortoiseshell, tin from Cornwall, copper and silver, producing objects decorated with all kinds of figures—men, animals, insects, flowers, foliage—or anything else that is in demand or may inspire the visitors to

Late nineteenth century Spa nécessaire painted with flowers and varnished. It opens to reveal two spools, a needlecase and a thimble. *Author's collection*

buy, for there are few places where similar objects are made. The technique of the local craftsmen is improving every day.

The souvenir ware flourished and the Spa shops were full of it, mostly decorated in the 'Indian manner', that is, in imitation Chinese lacquer. An important lacquer industry developed in Spa, and lacquer objects were made non-stop between 1690 and 1725, usually with a black background decorated with all kinds of Chinese motifs. They were also made with red, blue, green and yellow backgrounds. The Spa lacquer industry owed a lot to its most famous craftsman, Gérard Dagly, who had invented the formula of the famous Spa varnish. He had been born in Spa in 1665 and was apprenticed very young in the souvenir trade. He became so good at it that with his brother Jacques he went to work at the court of Frederick I, Elector of Brandenburg. Dagly left the Prussian court in 1713 when Frederick-William came to the throne. When he died in Binsfeld, Germany, in January 1715, his brother Jacques was appointed director of the lacquer workshop in the French state factory of Gobelins in Paris, before he returned to Spa to start his own workshop at 'The White Pigeon', where for years he continued to make souvenirs.

Writing in Amsterdam in 1735, an anonymous author could claim that the Spa shops were full of delightful lacquered objects of all kinds, decorated with miniatures representing scenes from Ovid's *Metamorphoses*—card-boxes, watch-cases, fruit baskets, snuff-boxes—all made in many different styles and techniques. Dagly, says the author, 'at the sign of the White Pigeon, produces the best water- and fire-proof varnish. We discovered that he had an excellent aptitude for painting fruit and Chinese and Japanese figures, always perfect, whether flat or in relief.' From the end of the seventeenth century onwards, Spa produced large dressing-cases in lacquer, which contained compartments and boxes of various sizes. According to one contemporary document, these boxes were meant to hold cosmetics, dressing accessories, toothpicks, powder, patches, one inkpot, two small candle-holders in turned wood and all 'the *necessary tools for sewing and embroidering*'.

Spa was frequented by all the most important people. Peter the Great of Russia was a visitor in 1717 and bought many souvenirs, including large panels in imitation lacquer which he bought from

Tiny workbox in Scottish Mauchline ware, transfer decorated with a view of the Belgian resort of Dinant.

Dagly—enough to decorate a whole room. He even took a Spa craftsman back to Russia with him, to help him start a souvenir trade in Olonets. Spa was quite used to crowned heads: amongst many others, Alexander Farnese had been twice, in 1578 and in 1599, and Christina of Sweden and Charles II of England were there in 1654—all returning home laden with souvenirs for their friends.

But then fashions changed, and the production of lacquer goods came to an end after the first quarter of the eighteenth century. The Spa painters started decorating their boxes with scenes drawn in Chinese ink, on backgrounds of various colours. Combination dressing- sewing- writing-cases continued to be made throughout the century and Spa produced *boîtes à ouvrages* (sewing boxes), often fully equipped with sewing implements and tools for lace-making or for embroidering, most of them in bone or ivory. The craftsmen of the little town also made beautifully painted bodkin-cases, needle-cases, pincushions, winders in the form of little towers—all decorated with hand-painted designs of flowers, birds and scenes, and always very bright and charming, with mottoes and declarations of love. They also made wooden darning eggs decorated with birds, flowers and mottoes. Eighteenth-century workboxes were decorated in Chinese ink with views from Spa and the neighbouring countryside. Some were decorated with religious scenes on a yellow background, others with landscapes on brown or natural wood backgrounds. There was something to suit all tastes—in fact there is absolutely no end to the variety of decorations one can find on Spa workboxes and other sewing accessories of the period. Some of the nicest workboxes were fitted with a drawer at the bottom containing spools, while the box itself was fully equipped with mirror, pincushion, silk-winders, needle- and thimble-cases. At the end of the eighteenth century, the workboxes began to be fitted with a pincushion lid.

In 1787 a Scottish nobleman, Lord Gardenston, arrived in Spa;

Lord Gardenston had created the village of Laurencekirk in eastern Scotland. While he was in Spa he visited one of the most famous shops there, the 'Dolphin', owned by the great artist Antoine Leloup, where he met a certain Vincent Brixhe, who had been employed by Leloup for the past twenty years. Brixhe had been born in Spa in 1756, the son of Joseph-Thomas Brixhe, who was well known for his paintings in Chinese ink. Following the example of Peter the Great and the Elector of Brandenburg, Lord Gardenston took Vincent Brixhe back with him to Scotland, to settle him in Laurencekirk where, according to his contract, he was to stay for three years, at £30 a year plus £5 for each apprentice he taught. According to Lord Gardenston Brixhe was familiar with all branches of the art, and particularly talented at painting flowers and imitation marble chaffers. It seems that Brixhe's contract was renewed and he never went back to Spa. And this is the story of how the famous Scottish souvenir ware industry was in fact started by a Spa man. It explains why the people of Spa did not understand for many years why the oldest Scottish boxes from Laurencekirk looked exactly like the Spa ones from the end of the eighteenth century. Even the wood used—plane—was the same, as well as the decoration, the same subjects being used in Scotland as in Spa.

Spa was at the height of its success when Brixhe was busy teaching the Scots. By 1780 a good hundred kings and princes had stayed in the town, including Gustav III of Sweden and the Duke of Orleans. The King of Sweden did not care for the waters, but, like many others, he spent his time gambling at the casino. The next year Joseph II, Emperor of Austria, was in Spa, and he declared it the 'café of Europe'. The local people were delighted, and they were doing a roaring trade in souvenirs too. At this time Spa was still producing all kinds of boxes and other trinkets decorated with scenes in Chinese ink, sometimes in black but also in blue and green. All kinds of sewing tools were being manufactured—workboxes, needle-cases, thimble-cases and winders—all decorated with scenes in the manner of the French school of painting. At the end of the century many objects were painted in gouache, with flowers, fruit, vases of flowers and garlands in the Louis XVI style. Fables and allegories flourished, views from Spa in bright colours in cartouches or on a monochrome ground imitating marble or tortoiseshell. And yet more sewing tools were produced in this style—workboxes, pincushions, needle-holders, pin-holders, darning eggs, silk-winders, lace tools, spool-boxes and combination needle- and thimble-holders.

Napoleon's Empire dealt a harsh blow to the Spa souvenir industry; no one rushed to Spa any more, and for a few years the great Spa hotels were deserted. A few families continued to make wooden souvenirs, but the high quality was not always maintained. Boxes of the period are sometimes decorated with engravings or lithographs glued to the wood and then varnished. But business picked up again after the Battle of Waterloo. The Duke of Wellington and Alexander I of Russia visited the town, and beautiful boxes and sewing equipment were made again, this time decorated with copies of works by painters such as Landseer, David Teniers and Wouwerman. Workboxes were bigger than before, with small compartments inside with lids decorated with scenes to match the outer lid. Sewing tools continued to be made until roughly the beginning of the First World War. Today one can still find such items as needle-cases, winders, workboxes, pincushions of various types, needle-books and darning-eggs. But after some three hundred years of success, at the end of the nineteenth century the industry was practically finished.

Spa souvenirs are becoming rarer and rarer in Belgium, where they have all been collected, but beautiful examples can be found just about anywhere else, and many a fine box has turned up in London, Edinburgh, Paris, Madrid and other big European cities. A splendid nineteenth-century Spa workbox was even found, complete with implements, in the Portobello Road. For the Spa souvenirs were made for the visitors of Spa, most of whom were foreigners who took the souvenirs back home.

Scottish souvenir ware

The Scottish souvenir ware industry owes much to the town of Spa

Egg-shaped nécessaire in Scottish Mauchline ware, containing a double spool, a thimble and a needle holder.

for, as we have seen, it was from Spa that Lord Gardenston took Vincent Brixhe to Laurencekirk to start the Scottish industry there. The first Laurencekirk boxes resemble the Spa ones down to the last detail. Even the well known Spa motif of a dog chasing a rat was reproduced in Scotland. The varnish, if analysed, would most likely turn out to be identical to Spa varnish, for the formula was known. And the wood used for the earliest boxes was plane, as in Spa. Understandably enough, Vincent Brixhe continued to make in Scotland what he had always made in Spa, and he taught his apprentices everything he knew: the methods and traditions of Spa which could be traced back to the sixteenth century.

The Spa varnishing process, used there for more than a hundred years, took a very long time: between fifteen and thirty coats had to be applied before polishing with ground flint. And the pen and ink decoration popular in Spa for a few decades found its way to Scotland; even the trees in pen and ink on the first Laurencekirk boxes look exactly like the trees drawn by Antoine Leloup, Brixhe's employer in Spa. The scenes painted on the Laurencekirk snuff-boxes did become more and more Scottish, although all kinds of hunting scenes reproduced on early boxes were to be found in Spa a long time before. The real change occurred when the Laurencekirk snuff-boxes were fitted with the famous Scottish secret hinges — hinges of wood which were almost invisible. Some experts think that the first to commercialize the secret hinge boxes was a certain Charles Steven, but in any event it was certainly a nineteenth-century innovation, introduced a long time after Brixhe's arrival in Scotland.

In 1807 only two artists were employed by the Laurencekirk industry, while Spa, at its lowest ebb under the Empire, had some seventy-five artists still working. Laurencekirk diversified at the beginning of the nineteenth century into tea-boxes and other fitted boxes, but never made any sewing-boxes or sewing tools. The business ceased completely somewhere around 1865. But the idea behind it, together with the secret hinge, had shifted to the west of Scotland. Around 1800 William Crawford from Cumnock in Ayrshire made boxes along the Laurencekirk lines, and by 1825 quite a lot of other makers, not only in Cumnock but in nearby villages like Auchinleck, Catrine and Mauchline, were in the box business. By 1845 only one

Scottish souvenir
spoolbox, with a
pincushion on the lid.

firm was left—that of the Smith family in Mauchline, which had
started around 1810. And it was not until 1820 that the first boxes
decorated in tartan started to appear.

In 1845 nobody in Scotland had ever thought of making anything
useful for a needlewoman, not even a pincushion. The time was
ripe for the Smiths, who had done well with their tartan ware, to
start making their bodkin-cases, knitting needle cases, needle-books,
pincushions and workboxes. But they never made worktables. Like
the other firms from Ayrshire, they had started by making snuff-
boxes in the Spa style, painted and highly polished. In 1829 the
Smiths opened a warehouse in Birmingham, then a workshop to
make Scottish souvenir ware which never saw Scotland. The two
brothers, William and Andrew, went their separate ways, but they
both continued to make ladies' workboxes, needle-cases and a
variety of other trinkets 'beautifully and correctly painted'.

Both brothers made tartan ware, and both mechanized the process. Until then their boxes had always been painted with gouache,
exactly as in Spa. Tartan ware had at first been painted by hand,
but mechanization substituted a printed sheet of paper glued to the
wood surface in such a way that it was practically impossible to
detect it. From 1845 they made what is now called their transfer
ware on sycamore. The transfer plates were made everywhere—in
London, Birmingham, Sheffield, but never in Scotland. This famous
sycamore ware, always decorated with black transfers, showed
scenes from Scotland, England and Wales, but also from Belgium,
France, Germany and Holland, as they were sold in quantity to all
popular continental tourist centres and seaside resorts. They can
therefore be found today in any European country, very often in
antique markets and in junk shops, where people rarely know what
they are. Who would guess that a needle-case decorated with a view

of a well known Belgian department store could be Scottish? Who in France would think that a pincushion decorated with a view of old Deauville could be Scottish? One can find many needle tools in Scottish souvenir ware, but those still around today are not necessarily old, as Smith's managed to survive until 1937.

Tunbridge Wells souvenir ware

Tunbridge Wells in Kent started attracting tourists as early as the seventeenth century, when the curative power of its spring water was discovered. People went there as others went to Spa, thinking the water would definitely cure them of their illnesses. It is most likely that Tunbridge Wells produced some kind of souvenir ware at an early date, but unfortunately it has not been possible to determine what exactly was sold in the Tunbridge shops before the nineteenth century. Strangely, no records have survived. If the ware had been very famous it would surely have been mentioned somewhere, and some pieces would have come down to us. All we do know is that 'curious wooden ware' was sold in the town at the end of the seventeenth century. 'Curious wooden ware' could be anything at all, and as a lot more people went to Tunbridge Wells during the eighteenth century, one might imagine that at least items from that period would have survived or left traces. But it is difficult to find out what was being sold to visitors to the famous spa town. There is a clue in the *History of Tunbridge Wells*, written in 1766 by one Benge Burr, in which he mentions that 'the trade of Tunbridge Wells is similar to that of Spa in Germany and chiefly consists in a variety of toys in wood, such as tea-chests, dressing-boxes, snuff-boxes, punch ladles and numerous other articles of the same kind.'

Benge Burr must have been quite bad at geography, or he would have known that Spa was not in Germany at the time, but in the Austrian Low Countries. His description leaves all possible doubts. If the Tunbridge Wells souvenirs were similar to those sold in Spa, they must have been in highly varnished hand-painted wood. As Benge Burr mentions in his book that they also made 'a prodigious variety of the prettiest ornamental inlays that can be imagined' and used all kinds of woods such as holly, cherry, plum, yew and sycamore, one can only conclude that two kinds of souvenir ware were sold in Tunbridge Wells—some hand-painted as in Spa, some made in marquetry. So it seems that, although initially Tunbridge ware owed something to Spa, from the end of the eighteenth century the Tunbridge craftsmen adopted a style unknown in Spa, producing all kinds of boxes and trinkets in real marquetry, and using, as decorative motifs, the Vandyke pattern (a zigzag design of alternating woods) and the cube pattern (fine bands of light and dark woods to give a three-dimensional impression).

In the eighteenth century, Tunbridge Wells produced dressing-cases and workboxes, but none have been reported anywhere. Objects in Vandyke and cube patterns were made until about 1830, when the Tunbridge firms discovered yet another way of decorating their ware. The new method was the easily recognizable grain technique. Bunches of thin sticks were glued together lengthways, and, when dry, cut in slices and glued on to paper before being veneered on to a wooden surface. From then on the craftsmen of Tunbridge produced a great variety of designs, always unique as no single one could be reproduced a second time. A variation appeared in the 1860s—stickwork. Instead of slicing the wood horizontally, it was turned on a lathe, the patterns this time running lengthwise. Only

Tunbridge ware worktable of great beauty, made circa 1878 by Nienhaus. *Courtesy of the Victoria and Albert Museum*

small items were made with this technique.

Tunbridge ware, in stickwork and end grain, was produced all through the nineteenth century—to the great delight of today's collectors. But exactly what happened in Spa also happened in Tunbridge Wells, and the once great souvenir business declined until by the beginning of the First World War it was practically at an end. In both cases a few diehards tried to keep up the good work after the Armistice, but to no avail, and the last makers disappeared one by one in the 1920s. A minor point of similarity between Tunbridge Wells and Spa is that both had the idea, during the last century, of soaking the wood in spring water before using it. But in both cases the idea was found to be not worth pursuing: the oak turned greenish, the sycamore a dirty grey.

The simple boxes designed in the cube or Vandyke patterns gave way, around 1830, to more intricate decorations, such as pictures of local places surrounded by one or two borders of flowers and leaves. From the 1840s the pictures were copies of the embroidery known as Berlin woolwork, and probably the best ever made in Tunbridge. These famous mosaic pictures were not always scenes and buildings of the town and neighbouring countryside, but of other places in Britain as well.

All through the nineteenth century, Tunbridge produced quite a number of needlework tools, and of a greater variety than the other souvenir ware industries. Tunbridge, for instance, was the only one to produce beautiful sewing-clamps. And there is no end to the list of sewing tools—needle-cases, pin-boxes, silk-winders, glove-menders, thimble-cases, and so on. Tunbridge is the only place to have produced pin-tables, the cushion being located between the two leaves of the top. One can find button-boxes, cotton-boxes, wax- and emery-holders, needle-books, darning-eggs, fan-shaped pincushions, silk-skein holders, pin poppets (made in the shape of a doll), reel-boxes, sewing compendiums, tape-measure cases, thread-waxers, silk-ball holders—all in the famous Tunbridge marquetry. It also produced some extraordinarily beautiful work-boxes and worktables, which are quite rare today and would fetch a high price anywhere. Tunbridge probably produced more sewing tools than all the other souvenir ware industries, and in a much greater variety.

9 MINIATURE SEWING TOOLS

If most sewing tools of the past are still being sold at a reasonable price, others are now very highly priced and out of most people's reach. It would be a very expensive proposition, for instance, to try to buy a French eighteenth-century worktable or even a nineteenth-century Tunbridge ware specimen, if one could be found. And some lavishly decorated nineteenth-century work-boxes, whether from Germany, Italy, France or Britain, still command a high price. Although the modest collector would not dream of owning such expensive antiques, he can always start a collection of miniature sewing tools—the sort that were made for little girls of long ago or those even smaller ones that were meant for dolls' houses.

Assembling a good collection of miniature sewing tools still requires a certain amount of patience and money, as the old toys that were formerly discarded and thrown into the dustbin are now collectors' pieces, as everyone knows. Sewing tool collectors would not usually contemplate buying a real sewing machine made at the end of the last century, for it requires too much space. But they can very well get hold of a miniature machine, a toy one, cheap to buy and easy to display. These were made from about 1875 until well into this century, and many have survived. They are usually very elaborate, decorated more often than not with gold designs printed on a black background. Some are just painted green or grey, or even red like the Vulcan Minor sewing machines made for little girls between the two world wars. Some of the cheap models, made of tin and very light, produced a chain-stitch only. Some better quality, heavier models make between two and four running stitches at each turn of the wheel. Two types can be found today—the foot-operated or treadle type, a very rare toy today, and the table model, driven by a manually operated wheel. Like many other toys of long

Miniature sewing machine by Singer, made in the late nineteenth century, complete with its own container.

ago, most of these sewing machines were produced in Germany and exported all over the world. Many were made by the firm of F. W. Müller of Berlin. Some toy experts maintain that about twenty different models were made before the First World War.

In the cheaper range one can still find the smallest sewing machines of all, those beautiful miniatures made for dolls' houses. In most old dolls' houses one finds any of various models of the two main types, the table and the treadle. These tiny sewing machines were first produced just after 1875, not very long after the real sewing machine became universally available. Although the toy sewing machines are actual working models, the dolls' house machines are unable to produce a stitch, even if some parts are moving and give the illusion of working.

Beautiful toy worktables, sold complete with implements to satisfy rich little girls of long ago, can still be found, once again in dolls' houses, made in various styles and in various types of wood. Some are real works of craftsmanship, while others were factory-made in cheap wood, the various pieces assembled with glue and then painted. Some of the rarest ones are artistically carved in ivory or bone, complete with fitments, scissors, needle-cases, silk-winders and tiny thimbles. Who made these wonderful tiny worktables is still a mystery!

From the beginning of the last century, lovely miniature sewing

Late Victorian doll's house sewing machine, measuring about two inches high.

nécessaires were made for little girls' dolls. All those famous Parisian ladies who produced the so-called 'fashion dolls' or *parisiennes*, such as Madame Huret, Madame Roehmer and Madame Simone, sold not only their beautiful leather dolls but trousseaux to go with them. And that included sewing *nécessaires* no longer than three centimetres, containing all kinds of sewing tools, such as thimbles, needle-cases, crochet hooks and scissors, most of them, except for the scissors, made of ivory. Some bigger *nécessaires* were made for little girls themselves to use, allowing them to imitate their mothers and play at sewing. Long ago, girls learned to sew when still very young, and many a sampler found today was made by a little girl of five or six years old.

Miniature workboxes, many in ivory, were also made for dolls' houses during the same period. Many miniature sewing tools can be found if one looks hard enough, and they are not necessarily included in worktables or boxes, but often separate. There is hardly a nineteenth-century dolls' house which did not contain a few pairs of metal scissors, sometimes even in silver, half an inch long or so. Microscopic thimbles are also often found, some made as toys and others as charms to be attached to bracelets. Quite a few of these tiny thimbles were made to be hidden, with other charms like a ring, a button or a small coin, in dumplings, mainly in Scotland.

All kinds of miniature sewing tools can be collected today, whether you own the original dolls' houses as well, or not. They are charming, delightful to look at, and often well made. They don't take up much room in the house, and make a pretty display in a cabinet or showcase.

Doll's house sewing table in carved ivory, circa 1890.

10 MISCELLANEOUS SEWING ACCESSORIES

Cotton- or silk-barrels

Cotton- or silk-barrels are to be found in many old workboxes. They were in the shape of a small barrel with a spindle inside, and a little hole at the side to let the thread through. These little barrels are not easy to find today, as many were simply discarded. Most of them are in wood and are insignificant in appearance, but some more luxurious types in ivory have been made. Some were made in Tunbridge ware, Spa ware and Scottish ware, and some very rare examples were carved out of mother-of-pearl.

Reel-boxes

Reel-boxes were often included in old workboxes. Sometimes a special drawer of the workbox was reserved for reels. But as women more often than not needed more than the four or six reels found in workboxes, separate boxes were also made which could hold up to twelve reels. The boxes, some of which are very beautiful, were fitted with little pegs to serve as stands for the reels. The thread could be pulled out of the box through tiny holes pierced through the side. Most of the reel-boxes found today in Britain or on the Continent are made of wood, sometimes painted and decorated. The most beautiful, once again, are in souvenir ware. Some fine marquetry ones were made in Tunbridge Wells during the nineteenth century, and Spa produced a few, always hand-painted with scenes or flowers, and highly varnished.

Reel-stands

Women always needed their collection of thread handy and ready

A very unusual reel-stand from the nineteenth century. *Museum of English Rural Life, Reading*

to use at any moment, so someone invented the reel-stand very soon after the invention and commercialization of the first wooden cotton-reels, in about 1830. It did not need to be the most ingenious invention, as all that was needed was an arrangement of little pegs suitable for holding the reels. From the start reel-stands were simply utilitarian objects, and never made in precious metals like so many other sewing tools of the past. Nobody would have thought to put them on display, for there was nothing particularly attractive about them. Basically, the reel-stand was composed of a round base fitted with a number of little pegs to hold the reels, very often with a central pedestal with the inevitable pincushion on top. In most cases the base revolved, making it easy for the needlewoman to select her thread without having to lift the stand off the table. Some models were made in brass and capable of holding up to twenty-four reels. All kinds of reel-stands were produced during the nineteenth and twentieth centuries, many being offered as advertisement give-aways by thread manufacturers, either direct to their customers or to shops.

Sewing-clamps

Before the days of the sewing machine, that is, until the second half of the last century, certain sewing tools were attached to a base

115

Beautifully carved wooden sewing clamp,
nineteenth century. *Museum of English Rural
Life, Reading*

which could be firmly clamped to a table, hence their name. Sewing-clamps were already in use during the eighteenth century, but most of the examples around today are of nineteenth-century vintage or even more modern than that. Most of the eighteenth-century clamps were made of iron, whereas the nineteenth-century ones were stamped out of tin, brass or bronze. Some rarer and more attractive specimens were carved in wood, bone or even ivory, and often inscribed, as they were given as presents; some rare ones were even made in silver.

Sewing-clamps were indispensable to the needlewoman of the past. Of course, quite a few different sewing-clamps were made and used. The first and simplest kind of clamp merely supported a pincushion. It was a good idea, for the usual pincushion is an elusive little item. Firmly held by the clamp, the pincushion was always in sight and securely trapped. The second type is the winding clamp, very useful for winding wool or thread without the help of a second person. Clamps meant to wind wool were fitted with large spools, and those with small spools were meant to wind thinner threads like silk or cotton. Another type was made for knotted fringe-work, and was fitted with round-topped pegs for supporting the maincord of the fringe.

But the commonest clamp was the hemming-clamp, which was to become obsolete once the sewing machine arrived on the scene. The hemming-clamp, too, was indispensable. Clamped to the table, it held the material firmly at one end, leaving the two hands of the tailor free for other tasks. The left hand could pull the material tight, while the right hand could first insert pins and then guide the needle and thread. It would have been very difficult indeed to try to hem without the help of a clamp. Most clamps were fitted with a pincushion, another splendid idea, for the sewer could reach the pins without difficulty and still hold the material with the left hand.

The most sought after of all clamps is the hemming-bird, which was made in various metals, including silver. Sometimes called the sewing-bird, it was the most attractive and most elaborate of all clamps. It was fitted with a bird of cast-iron, brass or silver, and the beak could be opened or closed by simply pressing down its tail. The material was held in the bird's beak until you wanted to release it. The sewing-bird was also practically always fitted with one or sometimes two pincushions. It began to be popular in Europe and America at the very beginning of the nineteenth century, and nobody has ever discovered who was the clever inventor.

Beautifu humming bird sewing clamp, mid-nineteenth century. *Courtesy of the Kay Shuttleworth Collection Trust*

Sewing-magnets

It is difficult to determine whether the sewing-magnet started to be used in the eighteenth or the nineteenth century. Whatever the case, generations of tailors, seamstresses and needlewomen have used a magnet to pick up needles and pins from the floor. It was a sound idea, because pins and needles, particularly en masse, are notoriously difficult to pick up. Even today most professional tailors and seamstresses still use a magnet. The usual kind was in the shape of a horseshoe, painted red except for the two tips. But many interesting magnets were made for the needlewoman, often of the novelty type and sold in souvenir shops. This kind of magnet was usually round and fitted with various sorts of fancy-shaped handles. Magnets came in the most unusual containers—in fact, anything that could be attached to a string or a chain. They have appeared in the shape of little turrets, lurked at the bottom of small statuettes or in bells, or even in a bell-shaped holder surmounted by a small glass ball containing a figure of the Virgin Mary. Sewing magnets of the novelty type often escape the attention of collectors, because they fail to realize that a magnet is hidden under the handle. Although fancy sewing-magnets don't look like magnets, they are well worth looking for.

Shuttles

The shuttle is a very ancient instrument used by weavers to pass the crosswise thread through the vertical threads of their canvas. The French called the shuttle a *navette* because it always had the shape of a ship, and the English word comes from the Old English *scytel*, meaning dart or arrow. This very modest instrument, always made in wood and without any particular decoration, managed to find its way into the parlours and boudoirs of the eighteenth century, when the ladies, always keen on needlework, discovered that it could be used to make a kind of lace. To find a good definition of the shuttle, let us turn to an eighteenth-century dictionary, the *Dictionnaire Critique et Pittoresque* which was published in 1768, when shuttles were widely used throughout Europe. The

Four styles of shuttle. From left to right: in plain ivory; modern shuttle with removable reel for winding on a sewing machine; mid-Victorian tatting shuttle in horn inlaid with mother-of-pearl flowers; tortoiseshell shuttle. *Courtesy of the Kay Shuttleworth Collection Trust*

anonymous writer tells us that a shuttle is 'a small instrument the shape of a ship, in mother-of-pearl or gold, used by the ladies to make knots, since it is indecent to use needle or spindle.' We may wonder exactly why it was 'indecent' in eighteenth-century Paris to use a simple needle, unless it was in the old sense of 'unbecoming' for a lady of fashion.

These shuttles were made not only in mother-of-pearl and gold but also in ivory, silver and gilt. Lazare Duvaux, the Paris dealer, reported in his accounts book that on 4th November, 1755, he sold to Madame de Pompadour 'a shuttle in gold, enamelled' for the sum of £600. Shuttles are reported in many documents; a well known newspaper published in Paris carried in its advertisements pages on 31st January, 1765, the announcement that someone had lost at, or on the way out of, the Comédie Française 'a Marly bag containing a Burgos shuttle, mounted in gold'. It would seem that that particular shuttle was imported from Spain. On 4th February, 1765, the same newspaper asked anyone finding the following to bring it back to Georges, a famous jeweller located on the quai des Orfèvres—'a gold shuttle in openwork, decorated with bronze-coloured silk, in a rose-coloured taffeta bag, embroidered with silver thread'. And Georges, of course, promised a reward to the finder.

119

It seems that a lot of shuttles were getting lost in Paris, for on 11th May, 1767, the Countess of Rancs, living in the rue d'Enfer, was also offering a reward to anyone who would return to her 'a gold shuttle in openwork, decorated in the middle with the symbols of love, in gold of various colours'.

Shuttles were so beautiful and precious that the rich ladies of the eighteenth century used to give them as presents to their friends. Most of them were decorated with good taste and highly valued, and some were already in collections. The best were gorgeous beyond belief. When the property of the Duke of Lorraine, Governor of the Low Countries, was sold in Brussels in May, 1781, the sale catalogue recorded seventeen shuttles. They are vividly described, giving us a very good idea of what they must have looked like. Of the seventeen shuttles, two were in crystal, two in gold, five in tortoiseshell, three in mother-of-pearl, one in agate, one in petrified wood and one in amber mounted in gold.

Knotting was a popular pastime of eighteenth-century Europe. The knotting shuttles used in England were usually smaller than their French counterparts, and probably less ornate; the length of a shuttle was somewhere between ten and fifteen centimetres. The only problem with shuttles is that they were already being collected two hundred years ago, and a modern collector needs a great deal of luck to find one today. Another type, the tatting shuttle, replaced the knotting shuttle in the nineteenth century. The simplest ones were made of wood or cheap metal; they were not as lavishly decorated as the older knotting shuttles, but most of them were made in ivory, bone, tortoiseshell or mother-of-pearl.

Silk- and cotton-winders

In the old days, before thread started to be sold on wooden reels in about 1830, silk and cotton threads were sold in skeins, which caused problems with tangling. So the skeins had to be wound on to thread-winders. These are of many shapes and made in a great variety of materials including mother-of-pearl, tortoiseshell, ivory, bone, wood and cardboard. Basically, a silk or cotton-winder was a flat grooved surface, on which the thread could be wound. Providing it was grooved, it could have any shape: circular, rectangular, square—or it could be in the shape of a star or a flower. Many rectangular silk-winders, in beautifully carved mother-of-pearl, were imported from China and, as a rule, were found in Chinese lacquer workboxes, which were first imported at the end of the eighteenth century. Cotton-winders never ceased to be made, and thread is still sold today wound on a wooden or plastic reel. The nicest wooden ones were made by the souvenir ware manufacturers of Tunbridge Wells, Mauchline and Spa—these were hand-painted with scenes, and highly varnished.

Flat silk or cotton winders of various shapes, made from wood, bone and mother-of-pearl, all nineteenth century. *Courtesy of the Great Yarmouth Museums' Elizabethan House*

A bobbin cotton tree under a glass dome. The tree itself is in brass. circa 1870.
Courtesy of the Kay Shuttleworth Collection Trust

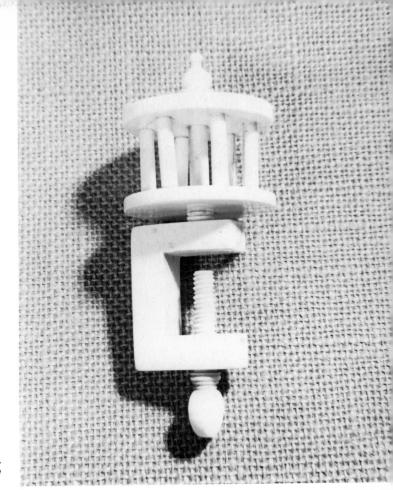

Unusual cotton and silk winder attached to a clamp. Probably Chinese, mid-nineteenth century. *Courtesy of the Kay Shuttleworth Collection Trust*

Four nineteenth century cotton, winders in wood, the left one being topped by a pincushion. *Courtesy of the Kay Shuttleworth Collection Trust*

123

Victorian tortoiseshell case containing wax for strengthening threads. *Courtesy of the Kay Shuttleworth Collection Trust*

Thread waxers

A long time ago threads were not mercerized and even-textured as they are today. If used just as they were sold, they would not pass smoothly through the material. So every needlewoman had a thread waxer handy when she was sewing. The waxer consisted of two discs between which a lump of beeswax was inserted, across which the thread would be drawn. Although they are collected, thread-waxers are not among the most appealing sewing implements one can find. Most of their circular discs were made of wood, but they are also found in ivory, mother-of-pearl and even bone.

Sewing-stilettoes

Stilettoes are very often found in old workboxes, as they were widely used during the last century, and probably also during the eighteenth. Most stilettoes consist of a sharp steel, brass or other metal point attached to a decorative handle in ivory, bone, mother-of-pearl, silver, or wood. Some are simply carved in ivory, bone or wood. Not many people know nowadays what they were used for. Needlewomen used the stilettoes to unpick stitches, to pierce eyelets in material, even to pierce button-holes or to pick out embroidery patterns. It is rather difficult to date stilettoes, as they are unmarked and have always been made the same way; it would be impossible, for example, to say if a stiletto dated from the beginning or the end of the nineteenth century. Today all kinds of stilettoes are worth collecting, providing they are decorative and in good condition; a collection of sewing tools would not be complete without a few.

124

Nineteenth century corkscrew stiletto with mother-of-pearl handle. *Courtesy of the Kay Shuttleworth Collection Trust*

Tape-measures

A household could not manage without at least one tape-measure. It was an indispensable aid to needlework, and most worktables and workboxes were sold with at least one included among their fittings. But tape-measures were of course also sold separately, and in all kinds of holders. What the collectors are usually after is not the tape itself, which is without much interest, but the holder.

Tape-measure holders could constitute a collection on their own, for so many different types were made—some really charming, even surprising, and in all kinds of materials. The earliest tape-measure holders simply contained a tape, usually a silk ribbon marked in inches or centimetres, which could be wound in by means of a handle; each container had a slit at the side to let the tape through. These holders were made of silver, ivory, all kinds of wood, cheap metals, tortoiseshell and mother-of-pearl, and later of early plastics like bakelite.

It is the form of the holders that attracts most people. The wind-in kind came in the shape of fruit (an apple or a pineapple), animals, birds, clocks, barrels, baskets, hatboxes, buildings, coaches. The most popular nineteenth-century holders were of the novelty kind, and in tourist resorts many were sold as souvenirs, just like pincushions and needle-cases. It was probably during the first years of this century that the holders were fitted with a spring mechanism which obviated the need to wind in the tape once it had been used. This kind was just as attractive as the wind-in type, and they too

125

Three typical nineteenth century tape measures, made in ivory or ivory and wood. *Folklore Museum, Tournai*

were produced in a great variety. They could take just about any form—a doll, an animal, a building, a flower, a ship, even the head of a woman. The materials remained the same for both types of holder, until the end of the nineteenth century when they started to be made in plastic, but, at the beginning, still in fancy shapes such as ships, flowers, hatboxes, windmills, dice. Slowly, however, the fancy shapes disappeared, and tape-measures were sold just as they were or in simple round boxes.

The tapes' ribbons, usually silk, had their measurements marked in ink, that is, before the end of the last century when they began to be printed. Some English silk ribbons made before the middle of the century were marked with little metal studs every $2\frac{1}{4}$ inches. But collectors should bear in mind that many tape-measure holders lost their tapes a long time ago, and may be overlooked because they look like any other container. Only the side slit gives the necessary clue.

Combined needlecase and yard tape measure of bone and vegetable ivory. The top incorporates a microscopic lens through which can be viewed miniature scenes of the Isle of Wight. Sold as a souvenir. *Courtesy of the Great Yarmouth Museums' Elizabethan House*

Tape measure from the 1930s, in metal with a decorative top in celluloid. *Margaret Kinnear Collection, Brussels*

Sewing-brooches

Sewing-brooches are sometimes found in old workboxes or in junk shops, and most people are not very sure what they were used for in the old days. In fact these brooches were very useful, and can be considered as much a sewing tool as a *nécessaire*. The brooch was composed of a small hollow cylinder, sometimes decorated with a semi-precious stone or simply engraved. It seems that some were made of silver, but most were produced in cheaper metals. The usefulness of the brooch lay in the fact that its main cylinder contained another cylinder, also hollow, which held needles and pins, and thread was wound round the inner cylinder itself. So the person wearing it had at her disposal a miniature *nécessaire*, allowing her to carry out repairs wherever she happened to be. Sewing-brooches were very popular before the First World War, but they are not easy to find because most of them were thrown away.

Darners

As the name implies, darners were used for darning and the favourite ones were always in the shape of an egg or a mushroom. Some egg-shaped darners were attached to a handle. They were usually made of wood, stone, glass, porcelain, pottery or horn. They come in various sizes, and some very tiny darning-eggs were made to darn gloves. But it is difficult to say whether any particular egg was made for darning or for some other purpose, as eggs have always been produced in all kinds of materials. Some stone ones were even made to be put in hens' nests as decoys. And after all, any hard egg could have been used for darning. So collecting darning-eggs is not always as easy as it might seem. The kind you can be sure were made for darning are the eggs or mushrooms with handles.

Select Bibliography

Victor Gay, *Glossaire d'archéologie du Moyen Age et de la Renaissance*, Paris 1887.

Henry Harvard, *Dictionnaire de l'ameublement et de la décoration*, Paris, 19th century, not dated.

Grand Dictionnaire Larousse du 20 ieme siècle.

Eleanor Johnson, *Needlework Tools*, London 1978.

Noel Riley, 'Tools of the needlewoman', *Antique Dealer and Collector's Guide*, October 1975.

ABC Decor, 'Les meubles, régionaux', November 1969.

Jane Toller, 'French prisoners of war work', *Antique Dealer and Collector's Guide*, July 1971.

Vivienne Becker, 'Scissor happy', *Antique Collector*, October 1976.

ABC Decor, 'Six siècles de ciseaux', November 1969.

Margaret Holland, 'Tunbridge Ware', *Antique Dealer and Collector's Guide*, August 1969.

Guillaume Janneau, *Meubles et Sièges*, Paris 1944.

Paul Guth, 'Les trois cents dés à coudre du baron Seillère', *Connaissance des Arts*, March 1956.

Encyclopedia Americana.

Encyclopedia of Antiques, Galahad Books, New York 1976.

Anne Clifford, *Cutsteel and Berlin Iron Jewellery*, Bath 1971.

'Trois siècles de bois de Spa', catalogue of exhibition held at the Musée de la Vie Walonne, Liège 1967.

Encyclopédie des styles d'hier et d'aujourd'hui, Paris 1969.

Savary des Bruslons, *Dictionnaire Universel du Commerce, d'histoire naturelle, des arts et métiers*, Paris 1723.